MW01716987

SHABUOT READER

VOLUME II

ARTICLES WITH INSIGHTS ON SHABUOT

IN MEMORY OF RABBI EZRA LABATON זצ״ל

Tebah

Copyright © 2014
Tebah Educational Services
N.Y., N.Y. 10001

Shabuot Reader

Volume 2

All rights reserved. Except as permitted under The U.S. Copyright Act of 1976, no part of this publication may be reproduced, distributed, or transmitted in any form or by any means, or stored in a database or retrieval system, without the prior written permission of the publisher.

For more information please contact:
Tebah Educational Services Inc.
by email at info@tebah.org.

Please send your donations (tax-deductible) to:
Tebah Educational Services
34 West 33rd Street, 2nd Floor
New York, NY 10001

Compiled and Edited by Raymond N. Habbaz

Cover artwork by Moses N. Sutton

ISBN: 978-0-9824875-5-6

Price: $9.95

Tebah Educational Services was founded with the recognition that present-day Judaism requires a greater focus on elucidating the intended meaning of the Biblical text as well as the values and guidelines for living that arise from a more complete understanding of it. Tebah's function is to develop, facilitate and publish various types of educational material, as well as school curricula that promote this goal.

Tebah Executive Committee

Publishing Committee

Eddie A. Ashkenazie * Ezra R. Barry

Joey I. Betesh * Rabbi Nathan Dweck

Norman E. Greenberg * Norman R. Greenberg

Raymond N. Habbaz * Aaron Senior

Jason Samstein * Moses N. Sutton

Tebah Executive Committee

Eli Benun * Abie Betesh

Morris N. Dweck * Rabbi Nathan Dweck

Eli D. Greenberg Esq. * Ricky Novick

Dr. Morris Shamah

Email: info@tebah.org

Internet: www.tebah.org

We gratefully acknowledge the following permissions:

Rabbi Alex Israel for "Megillat Ruth and the Shoftim Period" from www.alexisrael.org

Ktav Publishing House, Sephardic Institute and Tebah Educational Services for "Visiting Iniquity of Fathers upon Sons" and for "Reflections on Megillat Ruth" excerpted from *Recalling the Covenant* by Rabbi Moshe Shamah © 2011

Rabbisacks.org for "Wilderness and Revelation" by Rabbi Lord Jonathan Sacks © 2009

Judaic Seminar for Rabbi Ralph Tawil's "Haftarah of Shabuot's Second Day (Habaquq 2:20-3:19)" © 2002

The David Cardozo Academy for "Shavuot, Revelation and Learning" by Rabbi Nathan Lopes Cardozo © 2007

The Israel Koschitzky Virtual Beit Midrash of Yeshivat Har Etzion for "The Sinai Experience" by Rabbi Menachem Leibtag, and for "'Zachor' and 'Shamor' Were Uttered As One Word" by Rabbi Yoel Bin-Nun

Rabbi Yitzchak Etshalom and Torah.org for "*Mimahorat HaShabbat*" © 2009

In Memory of Rabbi Ezra Labaton זצ״ל

In the past few months numerous rabbis, scholars & community leaders have spoken about the enormous loss the Jewish world has sustained with the passing of Rabbi Ezra Labaton זצ״ל. He was special in the burgeoning modern traditional community and widely recognized as such.

An intellectual of the first order, whose doctorate – from Brandeis University – was in Jewish Philosophy and Bible, he regularly taught advanced classes in the wide spectrum of Judaic subjects. His specialty was pointing out the thrust of the text or concept under study in the world of practical application, thus inspiring his students to continually move forward in the realm of morals and ethics. His immediate audience was mostly composed of members of his congregation, but his larger goal – the apprehension of the values that are there to be drawn from the biblical text and their appropriate application to life – were the larger community. Thus his legacy extends far and wide.

As concerns congregational responsibilities the rabbi was superb. With a deep understanding of human nature he led many to successfully cope with difficulties, whether in personal life, family relationships or business matters. A master at conflict resolution, he was instrumental in settling many controversies. He constantly promoted Torah values in everything he did.

Despite his 7-day-a-week busy schedule, he managed to do justice to his responsibilities as husband, father and grandfather. His life-long עזר כנגדו, Emily, was truly his partner in all he did. She was often his sounding board for testing ideas; on occasion he would recommend to a rabbi discussing a recondite halakhic issue to speak with Emily, as it was a topic she was expert in.

Since its establishment in 2007, Tebah Educational Services has been one of the organizations dearest to the rabbi's heart. He volunteered to teach in our summer intern program, which significantly impacted the interns, and he wrote a number of articles for us. We are incorporating an article of his in the present volume. It is our pleasure to dedicate this issue in his memory.

Rabbi Moshe Shamah
June 2014

Sponsors

Eli and Monique Benun

Elliot and Freda Braha

Joseph and Sheila Cattan

Maney and Linda Douek

Morris and Julie Dweck

Joey and Raquel Franco

Eli and Lillian Haddad

The Mann Family

Sam and Susan Shamie

Joe and Adrienne Shamie

Louis and Adele Shamie

Sam and Nancy Sutton

Gabriel and Sophia Zeitouni

Tebah's Holiday Reader Series

High Holidays Reader

Pesah Reader

Purim Reader

Rosh Hashanah Reader

Shabuot Reader

Shabuot Reader: Volume II

Sukkot Reader

Sukkot Reader: Volume II

Tisha Be'ab Reader

Yom Kippur Reader

Table of Contents

About the Authors

Rabbi Yoel Bin-Nun is an Israeli educator and Rosh Yeshivah who has spearheaded the revolution in Tanakh-study in Israel, primarily at Yeshivat Har Etzion and the Herzog Teachers' College in Alon Shevut. He has written numerous articles and books on Tanakh, Jewish history, Jewish thought and halakhah. His shiurim can be found in English at www.vbm-torah.org, in Hebrew at www.etzion.org.il, and in *Megadim* publications.

Rabbi Nathan Lopes Cardozo, Founder and Dean of the David Cardozo Institute in Israel, is a prominent lecturer and prolific author who is world renowned for his highly original insights into Judaism. He holds a PhD in Philosophy.

Rabbi Yitzchak Etshalom attended Yeshivot Kerem b'Yavne, RIETS and Har Etzion before receiving his semikhah from the Chief Rabbinate of Jerusalem. He has been a dynamic educator in the Los Angeles area since returning there in 1985 and has been teaching on the internet since 1994. His first book, *Between the Lines of the Bible* was published by Yashar Books in 2006; volume 2 was published by Urim Press and the OU Press in 2012. Websites: www.etshalom.com & www.dafyomiyicc.org.

Rabbi Alex Israel is a beloved Tanakh lecturer and Rebbe, teaching at Jerusalem's finest Yeshivot and Midrashot. Educated at the London School of Economics and Yeshivat Har Etzion, he has published over 150 Tanach articles online. Rav Israel brings the Tanakh to life in his popular Israel tours, and volunteers for Tzohar Rabbinic organization, bridging the gap between the religious and secular in Israel. His book, *I Kings: Torn in Two*, was published by Koren Publishers in 2013. Website: www.alexisrael.org.

Rabbi Ezra Labaton z"l served as the rabbi of Congregation Magen David of West Deal for over 30 years. He received his semikhah from Rabbi J.B. Soloveitchik at Yeshiva University and completed his PhD thesis at Brandeis University in the field of biblical exegesis. He was a long-time student of Professor Nahum Sarna, who is recognized as one of the world's leading Bible scholars.

Rabbi Menachem Leibtag teaches Tanach at Yeshivat Har Etzion. His Tanakh classes, which emphasize biblical theme and structure, have opened his students' eyes to new dimensions within the text, while transmitting a deeper appreciation of Torah values. He initiated the Tanakh Study Center (www.tanach.org), his own comprehensive program for the study of Tanakh on the Internet.

Rabbi Lord Jonathan Sacks had been Chief Rabbi of the United Kingdom from 1991-2013. From 1984-1990 he served as principal of Jews' College. He received a PhD from Oxford University in Philosophy. In 2005 he was knighted by the queen of England. He has authored many works, including *Covenant & Conversation: A Weekly Reading of the Jewish Bible* (2009) and *The Great Partnership: God, Science and the Search For Meaning* (2011). Website: www.rabbisacks.org

Rabbi Moshe Shamah founded the Sephardic Institute in 1968 and continues as its director. He also serves as head rabbi of Sephardic Synagogue in Brooklyn, NY. He is the author of *Recalling the Covenant: A Contemporary Commentary on the Five Books of the Torah* (2011). Website: www.judaic.org

Rabbi Ralph Tawil received degrees from Columbia University and Yeshiva University and is a Jerusalem Fellow. He was the principal of the Hillel High School in Deal, NJ. He currently lives and teaches in Israel. His publication, *Shabbat-Table Talks: Volume 1*, was published by Tebah in 2013. Website: www.judaicseminar.org/tabletalk/1tabletalk.html.

Halakhot of Yom Tob[1]

Rabbi Moshe Shamah

I. Overview

The Torah prescribes six days of *yamim tobim* ("good days," festivals) in the course of a year:

* The first day of Pesah, Nissan 15
* The seventh day of Pesah, Nissan 21
* Shabu`ot, Sivan 6
* Rosh Hashanah, Tishri 1
* The first day of Sukkot, Tishri 15
* Shemini Asseret, the eighth day from the first day of Sukkot, Tishri 22

Yom Kippur (Tishri 10) is not counted amongst *yamim tobim* as it is not a celebratory day.

Each yom tob commemorates and celebrates a different feature of the nation of Israel's history and its relationship with God. Pesah commemorates God's redemption of the Israelites from bondage and the Exodus from Egypt; Shabu`ot corresponds with God's revelation at Mount Sinai and the establishment of the Covenant between Him and Israel; Rosh Hashanah (beginning of the new year) marks Divine kingship and human accountability; Sukkot recalls God's protection and providence over Israel.

In the Diaspora there are twelve yamim tobim each year: the first two and last two days of Pesah, two days of Shabu`ot, two days of Rosh Hashanah, the first two days of Sukkot and two days of Shemini Asseret.

The reason each yom tob is celebrated for two days in the Diaspora is as follows. In Mishnaic times the Israelites

---

[1] In matters of varying customs, these Halakhot follow the general Sephardic custom of the Aleppo-derived communities.

did not use a fixed calendar; rather, the *bet din hagadol* (the High Court) awaited witnesses to testify that they saw the new moon and then declared *rosh ḥodesh* (the advent of the new month) accordingly. In this manner the dates for the upcoming festivals were set. In lands outside Israel, there often was a doubt as to which of two possible days was declared the first of the month. This problem was a result of the fact that the lunar cycle is always approximately 29.5 days and it was possible that the first of the month could have been established on either of two possible days. (If witnesses did not arrive when expected, Rosh Hodesh was declared on the next day.) Because of the limited communications of the times, the doubt outside Israel was not always resolved by the time the festival arrived; in order to preserve the sanctity of the festivals, two days were observed for each.

In later Talmudic times, when a fixed calendar was used and there was no doubt as to when the first of the month occurred, the two day observance was retained out of concern that things may return to their previous state. Although modern communications renders the problem of the doubt inconceivable, legislation that was decreed by the High Court (Sanhedrin) cannot be annulled without the reconvening of another High Court, which has not been done these many centuries. Hopefully, we will merit its speedy reestablishment.

II. Prohibited and Permitted Work and Activities

Work and activities that are prohibited on Shabbat, whether from the Torah or by rabbinic enactment, are prohibited on yom tob, with certain major exceptions. Thus, writing, building, shearing, sewing, weaving, buying and selling, etc., are prohibited. However, the Torah permitted work of *okhel nefesh* on yom tob, that is, work that is performed for the purpose of eating on the day.

Thus, kneading, baking, cooking, slaughtering and salting meat, are permitted.

Actions that are part of the overall system of *okhel nefesh*, but which are not generally done for the purpose of eating on the day they are performed, such as harvesting, threshing, grinding and hunting, are prohibited.

Using fire and carrying from domain to domain are permitted. Since these are so pervasively intertwined with *okhel nefesh* they are permitted in and of themselves, even if not specifically done for eating, provided they are done for some benefit that will be derived during the day. Thus, heating water (opening the hot water faucet) to wash one's face, arms and legs is permitted. Heating water to wash the whole body at once, such as in the case of a shower, involves a technical question and should be limited to the second day only (when it is not Shabbat).

Generating a new fire, however, is prohibited, even if done for the purpose of preparing food. The permissibility of using fire requires a pre-existing fire. This halakhah is clear from the Talmud, Rambam and Shulhan Arukh. Hakham Obadiah Yosef z"l held that this prohibition includes striking a match. He acknowledges that several rabbis of stature in recent past generations considered a match as equivalent to extending a fire as it was deemed to contain fire in its tip. However, he states that this is not the view of the overwhelming majority of leading rabbis and that those accustomed to striking matches on yom tob should discontinue doing so.

One may turn on a gas range that has a pilot light as this does not involve generating a new fire but extending an extant fire. Many new gas ranges create a new fire when turned on and are the equivalent of striking a match, thus necessitating leaving a small flame on from before yom tob if one is interested in using it on the festival. If a non-

Jewish housekeeper kindles a gas range for her personal use, she may be asked to leave it on.

Wheeling a carriage, playing ball and roller skating are permitted on yom tob. Of course, if something breaks, it is prohibited to repair it on yom tob.

Muqṣeh applies to yom tob as to Shabbat; thus, although carrying is permitted on yom tob, carrying money or moving it, etc., is prohibited.

Cooking on one day of yom tob for the next day, whether the next day is a weekday, another yom tob or Shabbat, is prohibited. This applies to all permissible *melakhot* of yom tob. However, it is permitted to cook during the day for the upcoming evening meal if the meal will be started before nightfall. (This is common on Shabu`ot when many congregations pray arbit of the second day early). It is also permitted to cook dishes that children may partake of before sundown even if the majority of those dishes will be served at night.

When yom tob falls out on Friday, it is necessary to prepare an *`erub tabshilin* from before yom tob to permit cooking on Friday for Shabbat. The erub, comprising a cooked item such as a hard-boiled egg, and customarily a baked item such as a loaf of bread or matzah, is designated to be part of the Shabbat meal; thus, preparation for the Shabbat meal is considered to have begun before the onset of yom tob and in such a case the rabbis did not apply their prohibition of preparing for Shabbat. A berakhah "*Al Miṣvat `Erub*" is recited. The erub should not be eaten before Shabbat, and surely not before the conclusion of cooking on Friday for Shabbat; preferably, it should be part of the Shabbat meals, making *hamoṣi* on the loaf of bread. When yom tob falls on Thursday and Friday, the erub only permits cooking on Friday for Shabbat.

Although today we use a fixed calendar and know that the first day of yom tob is the actual day of the festival according to the Torah and the second day is from rabbinical enactment, both days are treated equally except for the following few exceptions:

1. It is permitted to engage in burying the dead on the second day, performing all the work that is necessary.

2. The rabbinic prohibitions associated with *refu'ah* (therapeutic practices and medications) that are applicable on Shabbat for someone who is not in a life-threatening condition do not apply to the second day of yom tob.

3. In accordance with the famous rule that governs doubtful issues in halakhah, doubts in halakhah concerning matters of the first day are generally resolved strictly while those of the second day are resolved leniently.

The first two exceptions do not apply to the two days of Rosh Hashanah.

III. Candle Lighting, Qiddush and Habdalah

Candles (or oil lamps) are lit for yom tob, customarily by the woman of the home just as is the case for Shabbat; the berakhah is "*Lehadliq Ner Shel Yom Tob.*" *Sheheḥeyanu* should generally not be recited with candle-lighting as it is expected to be recited in *qiddush*. If candles were not lit before sundown they may be lit in the evening, since the use of fire is permitted on yom tob.

The evening *qiddush* of yom tob begins with the berakhah on wine, followed by a berakhah that includes mention of the particular festival. If it is also Shabbat, the wording of the festival *qiddush* is recited with the mention of Shabbat included. Except for the last two nights of Pesah (which do not commemorate a "newly arrived" festival), *sheheḥeyanu* is also recited in the *qiddush*. On Sukkot, if one is eating in a sukkah, the blessing of *Lesheb BaSukkah* is attached to the *qiddush*.

When the festival falls on Saturday night, *qiddush* includes *habdalah* (in such a case making a distinction between "holy" and "less-holy"). The first two berakhot are recited as usual for the festival, followed by the berakhah for fire (on a candle or oil lamp). Then the berakhah of *habdalah* is recited. If it is a yom tob that requires *sheheḥeyanu*, it is recited fifth. Fragrant spices are not included in *habdalah* on a festival.

At the conclusion of yom tob, even between yom tob and hol hamo`ed (the intermediate days of Pesah and Sukkot), *habdalah* on wine is recited except when Shabbat immediately follows the conclusion of yom tob. In the latter case, only the standard Friday night *qiddush* is recited, for it would be inappropriate to mention the "departure" of yom tob in the *qiddush* for Shabbat. In the *habdalah* at the conclusion of yom tob only two berakhot are recited - on wine and the standard *habdalah* berakhah that is recited on Saturday nights all year long.

IV. General Halakhot

It is a requirement to honor and enjoy yom tob. The Torah prescribes a special mitzvah to be joyous on the festival. One must make preparations for this purpose. Families eat together and guests are invited. In our happiness we are required to remember the lonely and needy and share our blessings with them. It is incumbent on all to make efforts to invite them to participate in our festive meals and to provide for their welfare.

Yom tob annuls the "*shib`ah*" for one who is "sitting" in mourning for a family member, including one sitting for father or mother. This applies only if the mourner sat at least a short time before the onset of the festival. Yom Kippur also annuls "*shib`ah*."

If someone passed away on the festival, the seven-day mourning period does not begin until after the conclusion of the complete festival, including hol hamo`ed. Until then, only restricted, private mourning is permitted. The second day of yom tob, when it concludes the festival, counts as day one since it is of rabbinical derivation and the individual did practice a degree of private mourning.

V. Prayers

In each amidah of yom tob it is necessary to recite the portion that reflects the particular festival. If one mistakenly prayed a weekday amidah without mentioning the holiday, he must repeat the amidah and recite the one for yom tob. Musaf is recited daily, including during hol hamo`ed. Tefillin are not donned on yom tob. A special psalm associated with the theme of the day is recited for each yom tob, evening and morning.

Hallel is recited on all yamim tobim except on Rosh Hashanah. On the first two days of Pesah, on Shabu`ot, and on all nine days of Sukkot-Shemini Asseret, it is complete Hallel with a berakhah; on the later days of Pesah it is recited without a berakhah.

Special portions are read from two *Sifre Torah*. On yamim tobim there are at least five `olim to the Torah plus maftir. The Torah is not read at minha (unless it happens to be Shabbat).

Ya`ale veyabo is recited in Birkat Hamazon. If one concluded Birkat Hamazon and realized he did not recite it, he does not repeat, except on the first night of Pesah and the first night of Sukkot in the sukkah, as on these two occasions the requirement to eat at least a *kazzayit* matzah on Pesah and a *kazzayit* bread in the sukkah on Sukkot is mandatory. If one realized he did not recite *ya`ale veyabo* after concluding the third berakhah but before beginning the fourth, he should make the relevant insertion as found in the *maḥzor*.

The Moment

Rabbi Ezra Labaton z"l

One could argue that the Ten Commandments (or better: Ten Pronouncements or Statements), given on *Har Sinai*, were the most important piece of legislation that the world has ever known. Certainly, it has outlived the ancient law codes of the Mesopotamians, Hittites, and Hammurabi– though these predated the Torah by five to eight hundred years. Is there any law code more famous? These Ten Commandments have formed the basic legislation of the entire Western world and has impacted strongly on at least three billion people (1.2 billion Moslems, 1.8 billion Christians) – fully half of the world's population. This code has changed the course of world civilization. That moment at *Har Sinai*, celebrated on the Holiday of *Shabu`ot*, should be seen and appreciated as the most important moment in human history. It is most appropriate to analyze the factors that made this law code and this moment so significant and so impactful.

First, we should point to the Torah's two internal characterizations of the Ten Commandments. These characterizations will be helpful in understanding why the Ten Commandments were so impactful. *Shemot* 30:15 describes the Ten Commandments as *Luhot Ha-edut* – The Tablets of Testimony. What are the implications of this designation? To what do they serve as witness? One would not be far off the mark in suggesting that these *Luhot* serve as witness to *Bore Olam*'s ongoing involvement and concern with the world He created. Not only is the Almighty the Creator and Sovereign, but He serves as Master Legislator as well. God is concerned enough to provide His creations with a proper legal system with which to govern – a legal system that intends to guide mankind towards a proper Messianic end. Further, this code of law – based on the Divine word – testifies to the absolute nature of the moral system He legislated. The Israelites, and by extension all of humanity, are to strive to live by these absolute Divine, moral and legal norms. Whether one sees these norms as "Natural law" implicit in the human heart, mind and soul, or as "Revealed legislation," these norms are rooted in Divine concern about human behavior and the absolute nature of God's moral legislation. *Har Sinai* testifies to this concern.

As well, *Shemot* 24:7 calls these Ten Commandments *Luhot Ha-berit* – The Tablets of the Covenant. This legislative act is viewed by Torah as a contractual/covenantal agreement between the Creator and the Israelites. We are to become His chosen people and He is to be our God (see *Shemot* 6:7). As a result, we are responsible for bringing these Divine norms to the attention of all others – of sanctifying His Name. God, in turn, will guarantee our ongoing vitality as a nation. "I shall be your God and you shall be My Nation," underscores the indissolvable bond – the contractual agreement – between the Israelite nation and the God of our forefathers. This everlasting relationship is rooted in the "berit" that was contracted at *Har Sinai*. These two terms, *Luhot Ha-edut* and *Luhot Ha-berit*, serve as the basis of this Divine-human relationship. The Ten Commandments, and this legal system, are the result of this encounter – cemented at *Sinai*. A holy moment indeed.

As such, these Ten Commandments have to be viewed as central in the relationship between *Am Yisrael* and *Haqadosh Barukh Hu*. A violation of the covenant (the golden calf) has to result in the smashing of these tablets (Moshe Rabbenu). Here, the violation is viewed not only as disloyalty to God, but also as a violation of one's contractual/covenantal obligations. No relationship is possible with this sort of violation and disloyalty.

Having established how Torah views these Commandments and their centrality in this Divine/human encounter, we now turn our attention to the geographical and environmental factors that define the moment of this experience. First, we note that the site chosen was the empty, barren desert of *Sinai.* One may raise the question: Why the desert? Why not give the Commandments in this or that country? Here, the Rabbis of the Midrash significantly point out that the desert is open and free to all. No one nation has sovereignty over the desert. So too, the law of *Bore Olam* is free and open to all. Other nations and individuals may avail themselves of the opportunity of binding themselves to the Creator by adopting this set of Divine legislation.

Next, the starkness of the desert is highlighted by the mountain chosen for this event. Unlike the Canaanites who chose the high and mighty *Har Hermon* as their "holy mountain," and unlike the Greeks who chose Mount Olympus as their "temple of the gods," *Haqadosh Barukh Hu* chose a small, nondescript mountain – barely noticeable – and immediately forgotten after the event. (Note: There is no intrinsic holiness to this *har* – it's only God's presence that sanctifies, and with the withdrawal of that Presence, no sanctity remains.) Even more to the point is the root of the name *Sinai.* The Biblical commentators see this name as rooted in the Hebrew word *sanui* – that which is hated and abandoned by one and all (despite the change in spelling). And the alternate name, *Har Horeb*, derives from the Hebrew word *Hurban* – devastation and destruction. This mountain – not a very pleasant place – did not welcome visitors, nor did it fascinate or attract because of its majestic bearing. God specifically chose this abandoned, avoided, stark, desolate mountain upon which to reveal these Ten Commandments. The focus had to be on the majestic presence of *Bore Olam*, revealing His Divine glory, and not on the mountain itself.

The natural elements also play a role in this revelatory moment. The Torah goes out of her way to describe these factors. Thunder and lightning, fire and brimstone, all serve to heighten the tension (Shemot 19:16) and establish the moment as unforgettable. The mountain itself is described as trembling with the presence of the Almighty descending upon the mountain – surrounded by clouds and smoke – all aflame. This moment was intended to last for an eternity and to shape a people into God's chosen. It had to be awe-inspiring – a spiritually uplifting, overwhelming moment. And it was. The Torah records the fear felt by the people and their words begging Moshe to speak, rather than the Creator – *pen-namut* (per chance we may die). Moshe attempts to allay their feelings of trepidation by noting that this moment was intended to strike a note of fear and trembling into their beings, so that they never conceive of violating the norms of the encounter.

The geography and natural elements all conspire to establish this moment as "The Moment" – a one-time event in human history. But it wasn't enough – more was necessary to establish The Moment. Prominent at the *Har Sinai* experience was the sound of the *shofar* (*Shemot* 19:16, 19; 20:16). One wonders why? What did this primitive sound symbolize to the Israelites at that moment? What images did it evoke? What feelings did it inspire? Prior to this moment, we don't have any record at all of the *shofar* as ritually or spiritually important.

Yet, the Torah goes out of her way to note again and again how prominent was this sound, along with the thunder that filled the heavens. Did the *shofar* strike fear into their hearts? *Amos* 3:6 asks rhetorically: "Is the *shofar* ever sounded in the city and the people not tremble?"

Evidently, at a later time, the *shofar*'s blasting signaled fear. Though this verse is spoken five hundred years after the Sinaitic moment, perhaps the *shofar* played the same role earlier? Or did the blasts of this instrument signal freedom to the ancient Israelites, as it does on Yom Kippur of the Jubilee year? (*Vayiqra* 25:9) Our Torah text does not enlighten us as to any of these options, leaving us guessing as to the true symbolic meaning of the *shofar* – though we are quite sure of its significance.

But this is not all. Along with the geographical, environmental and humanly initiated *shofar* blasts comes Moshe's demand that the people must prepare themselves for the great moment about to be experienced. Proper *hakhana* (preparation) only serves to intensify the feelings of anticipation. First, the people must self-sanctify by washing their clothes (*Shemot* 19:10). Though we are not told why sanctification comes about in this fashion, and why this was significant, perhaps it may be explained as symbolic of a new beginning. Next, they were prohibited from coming close to a woman (*Shemot* 19:15). Here, Moshe had lead them away from any physical sensations. The Moment must be viewed as purely spiritual. The focus is not to be on anything human, but exclusively on the Divine. And then, finally, on the third day, the Moment was to be experienced (*Shemot* 19:11). For the first time in human history, a throng of people – a nation transformed - shall stand witness to what no other nation ever witnessed.

Three thousand three hundred years later, the nation of Israel still commemorates and celebrates The Moment. How could it not? Passed on from that Moment - from father to son and mother to daughter - were the sights seen, the sounds heard, the emotions felt. This Moment was preserved in the collective unconscious heart, mind and soul of this nation.

Our legal system, the ethics and ritual that define us as a people, are all rooted in that Moment at *Har Sinai*. The Ten Commandments established the covenantal relationship between the Almighty and His Chosen Nation. Our task now stands to pass on the power of this Moment to the next generation, as it is to pass it on to the other member nations of the world – to the Creator's other children.

The Sinai Experience

Rabbi Menachem Leibtag

Although the obvious purpose of *Ma'amad Har Sinai* is that Bnei Yisrael receive the mitzvot, their experience during that revelation is of equal importance. To uncover the thematic significance of their experience, we must carefully examine the narrative that describes that event (19:1-25).

Chapter 19 can be divided into four distinct sections: I. Proposition (1-8); II. Preparation (9-15); III. Revelation (16-19); IV. Limitation (20-25).

As we will show, this division helps us understand the importance of each section.

I. The Proposition (1-8)

After arriving at Har Sinai (19:1-2), God summons Moshe to present Bnei Yisrael with the following proposition (19:4-6):

> If: "You will obey Me faithfully and keep My covenant..."
>
> Then: "You shall be to Me a '*mamlechet Kohanim vegoy kadosh'* [a kingdom of Priests and a holy nation]..."

It is not by chance that God's opening statement to Bnei Yisrael at Har Sinai begins with: "*im shamo'ah tishme'u bekoli*" – 'If you will truly obey Me.' As explained in the previous *shiurim*, it was precisely this call for obedience that Bnei Yisrael did not heed prior to their redemption. After the various incidents in the desert that helped build Bnei Yisrael's spiritual character, God must first verify that they are truly ready to receive the Torah.

In addition to confirming their total obedience, the second phrase in God's proposition – "*u'shmartem et beriti*", 'and you shall keep My covenant' – suggests that the time has come for Bnei Yisrael to fulfill the next stage of God's *covenant* with the Avot. As we explained numerous times in Sefer Breishit, the purpose of God's covenant with the Avot was for Bnei Yisrael to establish an ethical and just, model nation ("*mamlechet kohanim*") in Eretz Canaan that will represent Him. By keeping the mitzvot which they are about to receive, Bnei Yisrael can fulfill this Divine goal.

Therefore, Bnei Yisrael must receive the mitzvot *before* they enter the Land. As these mitzvot will be binding for all generations, they must be given in a covenantal ceremony.[1] A covenant, by its very nature, is only binding if both sides willingly agree. Therefore, the Torah must emphasize Bnei Yisrael's collective acceptance of this covenant (19:7-8).

II. Preparation (9-15)

After Bnei Yisrael accept God's proposition, they must prepare themselves for His *hitgalut* (revelation). First, God explains to Moshe that He plans to speak to the people using Moshe as an intermediary:

> And God said to Moshe, "I will come to you in a thick cloud in order that the people will hear when I speak with you..." then Moshe reported the people's words to God. (19:9)

The second half of this pasuk is very difficult. What "words of the people" did Moshe report?

It *cannot* refer to the people's acceptance of God's proposition, for that was already reported in the previous

---

[1] Note also that Matan Torah itself is referred to as a covenant; see Dvarim 4:13 & 5:2-3.

pasuk (see 19:8). More likely, it refers to the people's response to God's statement in the first half of that *pasuk*, i.e. that Moshe is to act as an intermediary. Unfortunately, the Torah does not tell us what that response was.

Rashi (quoting the *Mekhilta*) "fills in" the missing details of that response:

> We want to see our King, for one cannot compare hearing from a *shaliach* (an intermediary) to hearing directly from God Himself!

Rashi's explanation is based on God's response, as explained in the *pesukim* that follow:

> And God told Moshe, "Go to the people and get them ready... for on the third day God will reveal Himself in the sight of all the people on Har Sinai." (19:10-11)

Bnei Yisrael's response can be determined from the apparent change in God's plan as to how His revelation will take place. This change is implicit in the contradiction between 19:9 and 19:11:

- 19:9 implies that Moshe will act as an intermediary- from now on, referred to as **Plan A.**
- 19:11 implies that Bnei Yisrael themselves will *see* God - from now on, referred to as **Plan B**.

According to Plan B, Bnei Yisrael will hear the Commandments directly from God. Therefore, this "change of plan" requires that Bnei Yisrael reach even a higher level of spiritual readiness, as reflected in the three day preparation period (see 19:10-15).

Are Bnei Yisrael capable of reaching this level? Are they truly ready to witness God's Revelation in the manner that they requested? From the *pesukim* which follow, it is not clear that they were.

III. Revelation (16-19)

On the third day, Bnei Yisrael become fearful due to the thunder and lightning that precede God's approaching *hitgalut*. Apparently, the people remain in the camp instead of gathering at Har Sinai (see 19:16). Moshe himself must take them out of the camp towards God, to stand at the foot of the mountain (19:17). God reveals Himself in fire on Har Sinai, and the entire mountain is enveloped in a *thick cloud* of smoke (19:18).

Now that God has revealed Himself, i.e. He has descended on Har Sinai, the next *pasuk* should describe God's proclamation of the Ten Commandments. Let's examine that *pasuk* (19:19) carefully:

> The sound of the shofar grew louder and louder, Moshe spoke and God answered him "*bekol*".[2]

According to Rashi, this *pasuk* describes God's proclamation of the **first two** Commandments. The Mechilta (quoted by Ramban), also claims that this *pasuk* refers to *Matan Torah*. Thus, one could conclude that Bnei Yisrael actually heard the *dibrot* (at least the first two) directly from God, i.e. Plan B.

Ramban, together with many other commentators, argue that 19:19 does *not* describe *Matan Torah*, rather, it describes the nature of the conversation between God and Moshe regarding where everyone is to stand when *Matan Torah* takes place (19:20-25). From those *pesukim*, it is clear that only Moshe will witness the *shechina* at the **top** of the mountain [Plan A], while Bnei Yisrael are not permitted to *see*, lest they die:

---

[2] "*Bekol*" could be interpreted as either 'with His voice' or 'with thunder.'

> ...Go down and warn the people lest they break through toward God to see, and many of them will perish. (19:21)

Once again, Ramban prefers to keep the sequence of events according to the order of the *pesukim*, while Rashi is willing to "change" the order.

To better understand the *machloket* (controversy) between Rashi and Ramban, we must examine the last set of *pesukim* (19:20-25) that precede the Ten Commandments (20:1-14).

IV. Limitation (19:20-25)

The *pesukim* that follow seem to indicate another change in plan. All of a sudden, God decides to *limit* His revelation to the top of the Mountain:

> And God descended upon Mount Sinai to the **top** of the Mountain, then summoned Moshe to the **top** of the Mountain, and Moshe ascended. (19:20)

Since only Moshe can ascend, the people must be warned *once again* to keep their distance. Even the "*kohanim*" who apparently are permitted to come closer than others, receive a special warning (19:21-25).[3]

From these *pesukim*, it appears that God will reveal Himself to Moshe alone, and *not* to the entire nation. Has God reverted to Plan A (that Moshe is to act as an intermediary)? If so, why? If Plan B remains, why is God's revelation now limited to the **top** of the mountain? Could this be considered some sort of a compromise, perhaps Plan C?

---

[3] Note that 20:25 refers to Moshe conveying this warning to the people, and *not* to conveying the "*dibrot*," as commonly misunderstood.

A possible solution to this dilemma can be deduced from the change in 'person' that takes place between the second and third commandment.

V. The Ten Commandments – First or Third Person

The first two commandments (20:2-5) are written in first person, indicating that God conveyed them *directly* to the people [Plan B]. The last eight commandments (20:6-14) are written in third person, indicating a less direct form of communication, i.e. that Moshe conveyed them to the people [Plan A].[4]

This change of "person" between the second and third commandment supports Rashi's explanation in 19:19 that the people heard the first two commandments directly, i.e. the *pesukim* that describe God's limitation of His *shechinah* to the top of the mountain (19:20-24) take place in the middle of the Ten Commandments.

Ramban argues that the people heard *all* the commandments through Moshe (Plan A), i.e. *none* of the commandments were heard directly from God. According to Ramban, the people's fear of the thunder and lightning caused them to revert back to the original plan (see Ramban 20:15).

Ibn Ezra (20:15) takes an opposite approach. He maintains that the people heard all Ten Commandments directly from God [Plan B].

In the description of *Matan Torah* in Sefer Dvarim, we face a similar dilemma when attempting to determine precisely what happened:

> Face to face God spoke to you on the mountain out of the fire [Plan B]. I stood between God and you at that

---

[4] This reflects *Chazal*'s explanation: "*Anochi veLo Yihiyeh Lachem, mipi hagevurah shema'um,*" i.e. the first two commandments were heard directly from God (*Makkot* 24a). See also Chizkuni 20:2.

> time to convey God's words to you [Plan A], for you were afraid of the fire and did not go up the mountain. (Devarim 5:4-5)

Even though Rashi's interpretation appears to be the most logical, the other commentators also present very solid arguments. The *machloket* between the various commentators undoubtedly results from the ambiguity in the *pesukim* themselves.

Why can't the Torah be more precise about such an important detail of the most important event in our history?

VI. *Ahava* and *Yir'ah*

One could suggest that this ambiguity is intentional, as it reflects the very nature of man's encounter with the Divine.

Man, in search of God, finds himself in a dialectic. On the one hand, he must constantly strive to come as close to God as possible (*ahava* - the love of God). On the other hand, he must constantly be aware of God's greatness, and recognize his own shortcomings and unworthiness (*yir'ah* the fear of God), and thus keep his distance (see Dvarim 5:25-26.).

God's original plan for *Matan Torah* was "realistic." Realizing man's inability to directly confront the *shechinah*, God intends to use Moshe as an intermediary (Plan A). Bnei Yisrael, eager to become an active covenantal partner, desired to come as close as possible to Har Sinai. They themselves want to encounter the *shechina* directly.

Could God say **no** to this sincere expression of *ahavat Hashem*? On the other hand, answering **yes** could place the people in tremendous danger, for to be deserving, Bnei Yisrael must reach a very high level.

Plan A reflects reality, while Plan B reflects the ideal. One could suggest that by presenting the details in an ambiguous way, the Torah is emphasizing the need to be both realistic and idealistic at the same time.

VII. God Knows Best

Although God is aware that Bnei Yisrael are not capable of sustaining a complete encounter with the *shechinah*, nonetheless, He concedes to the people's request to hear the Commandments directly. Why?

One could compare this Divine encounter to a parent-child relationship. There are times when a child is growing up and he wishes to do something by himself. Although the child may not be capable of performing that act, his desire to accomplish is the key to his growth. A wise parent will allow his child to try, even though he knows that the child will fall. Better one recognize the limits of his capabilities on his own, than be told by others that he cannot accomplish.

A child's desire to grow should not be inhibited by an overprotective parent. On the other hand, a responsible parent must also know when to tell his child, "Stop!"

Likewise, God is aware that Bnei Yisrael do not deserve to encounter the Divine at the highest level, nevertheless He encourages them to aspire to their highest potential. As Bnei Yisrael struggle to maintain the proper balance between *ahava* and *yir'ah*, God must guide and Bnei Yisrael must strive.

When studying Parshat *Yitro*, what actually happened at *Ma'amad Har Sinai* remains unclear. What could have happened remains man's eternal challenge.

Visiting Iniquity of Fathers upon Sons[1]

Rabbi Moshe Shamah

I. A Jealous God

After prohibiting all forms of idolatry, the second commandment continues with the following: "For I, Hashem your God, am a jealous God" (Exod. 20:5). The attribute employed, קַנָּא, invokes imagery of an enraged husband resentful of his wife's directing her affections to another. Hashem's covenant with Israel – although at this point it may not as yet have fully addressed the issue of the nonexistence of other deities – requires faithfulness and exclusive loyalty to Him; infidelity is construed as provoking His wrath as it does that of a jealous husband. (Marriage imagery associated with the covenant is attested a number of times in Scripture.)

The verse continues: פֹּקֵד עֲוֹן אָבֹת עַל-בָּנִים וְגוֹ', "who visits the iniquity of fathers upon sons, upon the third and upon the fourth [generations] to those that hate Me, and who does kindness to the thousands [of generations] to those that love Me and keep My precepts."

Multigenerational retribution is attested four times in the Torah, in each instance connected with the most egregious of transgressions. In both Decalogue formulations it is invoked for idolatry. In Exodus 34:7, in the context of the reestablished covenant subsequent to the golden calf apostasy, Hashem includes multigenerational retribution among His attributes. In Numbers 14:18, Moses

---

[1] Reprinted with permission from "Parashat Yitro Part III" of Rabbi Shamah's book, *Recalling the Covenant* (Hoboken, NJ: Ktav, 2011), pp. 371-379.

cited it in his prayer for forgiveness following the nation's rejection of the promised land, also a major breach of the covenant. It appears that multigenerational retribution is only applicable to cases of major breaches of the covenant.

How is such retribution to be understood? Does God punish innocent children for the sins of their parents? If so, even if such a policy is to serve as a deterrent, can it be reconciled with the natural, almost intuitive, human definition of justice?

At the outset it must be emphasized that the concept of multigenerational retribution in the Torah refers exclusively to retribution meted out directly by the Deity in His own legal justice realm. Regarding measures dispensed by a human court, the Torah states: "Fathers shall not be put to death for sons, nor sons be put to death for fathers; a person shall be put to death only for his own sin" (Deut. 24:16). This verse refers to the realm of earthly administration of justice. It appears amid a cluster of human responsibilities and is formulated as a directive to a human court; indeed, a statement concerning the divine court of justice at that point in the text would be anomalous. The key verb יוּמְתוּ is elsewhere always employed for execution at human hands. King Amaziah quotes this verse as the legal source that prohibits execution of the sons of his father's assassins (2 Kings 14:5-6). Although speaking about the death penalty, this proscription has been understood as totally banning all human vicarious punishment.

Thus, in discussing "visits the iniquity of fathers upon sons," we are theorizing about what the Deity does in His realm. Whatever explanation we give does not affect the reality of things since it does not relate to any action that may be undertaken by human initiative.

II. A Major Qualification

The Talmud (*b. Sanh.* 27b; also see *b. Ber.* 7a) significantly diminishes the scope of God's punishment of "visits the iniquity of fathers upon sons." It construes it as only applicable when sons continue in the evil ways of their fathers. It cites a verse in the Leviticus execration that implies this principle: וְהַנִּשְׁאָרִים בָּכֶם יִמַּקּוּ בַּעֲוֹנָם...וְאַף בַּעֲוֹנֹת אֲבֹתָם אִתָּם יִמָּקּוּ ("And they that remain among you shall waste away in their sins…and even in the sins of their fathers that are with them shall they waste away" [Lev. 26:39]).

Although the Talmud does not cite it, some scholars detect this qualification in the Decalogue passage itself. The "visits iniquity" clause specifies לְשֹׂנְאָי ("to those that hate Me" [Exod. 20:5]). They view this as a reference to the sons that hate God, restricting retribution for fathers' sins to such children. Similarly, His kindnesses that extend to future generations לְאֹהֲבַי וּלְשֹׁמְרֵי מִצְוֹתָי ("to those who love Me and keep My commandments") also extends only to those children who maintain love for Him and are faithful to His commandments.

Others, however, understand "to those that hate Me" as referring to the sinning fathers, not their children. The syntax fits the fathers very well. Hashem warns: Do not engage in idolatry, for I am a jealous God who visits fathers' sins on their sons, for those (fathers) who hate Me. That would imply that the sins of those who do not hate Him (less severe sinners) are not visited upon their children. This supports the distinction pointed out in the previous section between the major and all other transgressions. Either way, "to those that hate Me" restricts the scope of "visits iniquity."

In the two non-Decalogue Torah attestations of "visits iniquity," the qualification "to those that hate Me" does not appear. The explanation may be that in those contexts "visits iniquity" is mentioned as one of a number of God's attributes, not focused on a specific sin or theoretical sinner and therefore not calling for a possible qualification of the attribute.

It appears that support may be found in Deutoronomy 7:9 for the view that the Decalogue's qualification "to those that hate Me" applies to the sinful fathers. That verse paraphrases the multigenerational reward statement of the Decalogue in standard chiastic fashion (with sequence reversal of the clauses): "to those who love Him and guard His commandments to a thousand generations." In this case, "those who love Him" clearly refers to the parents. Analogously, although multigenerational punishment does not appear in that passage, the Decalogue's statement "to those who hate Me" would presumably also refer to the parents. (That this verse speaks of a "thousand generations" in contrast to the Decalogue's "thousands" may be a result of the absence of the word "generations" in the Decalogue. Both mean "indefinitely.")

It appears that Jeremiah 32:18-19 supports the thesis that "visits iniquity" is restricted only to sons who continue in their father's sinful ways. In the first of these two verses the prophet cites Hashem's attribute of multigenerational reward and punishment and in the second he speaks of the principle of individual accountability.

> 18. Who does kindness to the thousandth (generation) and compensates the iniquity of fathers upon their sons after them....
>
> 19. ...whose eyes observe all the ways of men to give each according to his ways and according to the fruits of his doings.

In order that these verses not contradict one another – not to speak of complementing each another, which surely appears to be the intention – the first has been understood as referring to children who continue in the ways of their parents, the second to those who do not. The qualification need not be explicitly stated as these verses are within a context of the prophet speaking to God.

III. Interpretations

Concerning the matter of the justice of cross-generational retribution, many have found a "naturalistic" interpretation appealing. God created the world with a natural order that possesses a great degree of constancy and with the general effects of human behavior and tendencies as they are. Accordingly, consequences that ensue from this state of affairs may be considered as His doings. The reality of the world is that a man's evil behavior usually influences his children, causing them to commit fresh offenses. A sinner places the burden of his behavior upon his children and to some extent upon their children also. Thus, by virtue of being the author of the natural order, it can be said that God visits the iniquity of fathers on sons.

Although all may agree that this reflects the prevalent reality of the world as we experience it, many have considered it strained to assume that the Torah would translate so naturalistic a process – with its many exceptions – into so active and definite a verbal clause as "visits the iniquity of fathers upon sons." Also, why then should cross-generational retribution only apply against those who breach the covenant, as appears to be the case? In addition, how would naturalistic influences account for the huge dissimilarity between four generations of punishment for the sinners and thousands of generations of reward for the faithful, a point the Torah stresses? Some have answered that negative behavioral influences are only overwhelming when the father is a flagrant violator. It also is often the case that in old age – as they observe their progeny – sinners do not advocate the errant path that they had tread and in the course of several generations positive societal influences neutralize their impact. And the complex workings of human free will in resisting negative influences cannot be ignored.

M. D. Cassuto proposed a more refined naturalistic argument in the following comments:

> The verse is directed to the [concept of the] totality of the nation being a united entity throughout time. Since man, particularly an Israelite man, is grieved at the afflictions of his children and grandchildren more than at his own afflictions, Scripture issues a warning, in order to keep man distant from sin…it is possible that children and grandchildren will suffer as a consequence of their fathers' or grandfathers' sins. From the other angle, Scripture moves our hearts toward the love of God by the guarantee that the beneficent results of such love will endure in the life of the nation and will be imparted upon children, grandchildren and their descendants till thousands of generations. (Cassuto, *Commentary on Shemot*, p. 168 [author's translation])

He further stated:

> The covenant between God and Israel is the essence of the nation's identity and the foundation of its purpose. It is appropriate for every member of the nation to sacrifice a great deal for the opportunity to have this relationship with God. If the most potent way to ensure the viability of the covenant in Moses' time was for God to treat father and son to some degree as a single entity such that there is cross-generational reward and punishment, it is understandable.

It is incorrect to construe the above as viewing cross-generational punishment as a case of "the ends justify the means," punishing the son to benefit the father, which would set a precedent for a dangerous doctrine. As Cassuto interprets it, the system directly benefits everybody by providing a deterrent to all – sons usually are also fathers. In addition, even if the "natural order" interpretation is not accepted as the full intent of the Torah in this matter, it does describe a general evil that usually afflicts the sons of sinning fathers. Thus, God's meting out multigenerational punishment is a deterrent that would ultimately redound to the son's great advantage.

In any event, although the questions on a naturalistic interpretation seem to have been answered (especially since we are dealing only with God's guidelines for Himself and He would always ensure that justice be done), many have rejected naturalistic approaches in favor of a view that "visits iniquity" depicts an aspect of God's active dispensing of retribution.

Some have explained "visits the iniquity of fathers on sons" as associated with God's mercy. In Numbers 14:18, in Moses' prayer for forgiveness after the national transgression of refusing to go forward to the promised land, he includes the divine characteristic of "visits the iniquity of fathers on sons." This may perhaps be understood as asking Hashem in His mercy to spread the full measure of retribution through the generations, to allow the present generation the opportunity to live and mend its ways or at least to keep the covenant extant. In this way, the future generations would also benefit. However, such an interpretation does not seem to fit the Decalogue's tenor, where the statement is used to warn against idolatry.

The significance of four generations appears to be that an average, full lifespan usually extends through great-grandchildren. It is these descendants whom we assume the sinner cares about. The righteous, on the other hand, are different. They are not selfish and self-centered and are not limited in their concern to their immediate descendants. They identify with God's goal for the betterment of the world and care about the welfare of future generations, even very distant future generations. They are particularly concerned as regards their descendants, even thousands of generations later, those future people whom they caused to be born into the world. It is great satisfaction to the righteous to know that through their behavior they helped someone, that they participated with God in instilling goodness into the world, even if they do not specifically know who the recipients will be.

This subject of "visits iniquity" is part of the larger and perhaps most difficult issue in religion, that of theodicy – the fairness of God's system of dispensing reward and punishment. This matter was raised on several occasions by the prophets and discussed a number of times by the sages. Although it is not the primary topic of this study, several comments are in order.

IV. Additional Comments

In the Talmud, Rabbi Johanan in the name of Rabbi Jose states that Moses asked God to reveal to him why some righteous receive a favorable portion in life while other righteous suffer and why some wicked receive a favorable portion while other wicked suffer (*b. Ber.* 7a). Rabbi Johanan asserts that the answer God gave was that it depends on the father – a righteous person may suffer because of his wicked father, etc. The Talmud, in an אֲמַר מַר ("the master said") analysis stemming from a later generation, rejects the possibility that Rabbi Johanan ever transmitted such a view and provides a different explanation as to what God answered Moses. Those righteous who receive a favorable portion in life are completely righteous while the righteous who suffer are not completely righteous and the same principle applies in reverse to the wicked.

The reason the Talmud took the unusual step of rejecting the "tradition" received from Rabbi Johanan and imputed a totally different explanation to his statement was because it accepted as an axiom that "Hashem punishes sons for the sins of their fathers only when they continue in their fathers' ways." Accordingly, it assumed that the original formulation cited in the name of Rabbi Johanan that he quoted of Rabbi Jose had to be mistaken.

In that passage, Rabbi Meir is cited as disagreeing with the statement of Rabbi Johanan in the name of Rabbi Jose. He was of the opinion that Hashem never answered that question of Moses given that לֹא תוּכַל לִרְאֹת אֶת-פָּנָי, ("you cannot perceive My countenance" [Exod. 33:20]): the answer to Moses' question is a matter beyond human comprehension. These varying statements cannot be reconciled as the sages clearly had conflicting opinions.

In the Talmud and within classic rabbinic tradition there is the view that God sometimes visits the iniquity of parents even on innocent children, but only when those children are very young. For example, "Ribbi states: For the sin of violating one's vows, one's young children may die" (*b. Shabb*. 32b). Although the Talmud does not connect it to the clause "visits the iniquity of fathers on sons," some do view it as an application of it and of course only relevant for a violation in the sphere punishable by God.

The Rambam wrote: "There are transgressions for which the punishment is exacted from…one's young children, for a person's young children who do not yet have *da'at* (understanding) and did not reach the obligation of fulfilling the commandments are treated as the parent's possessions" (*Mishneh Torah*, Laws of Repentance 6:1).

Abarbanel summarizes what he considers the primary rabbinical view:

> [God "visits the iniquity of fathers upon sons"] when the sons are very young, before the age of accountability for their own actions, for they are then considered extensions of their fathers and may be punished for his sins...until the fourth generation, those that the original idolater may see in his lifetime...[for he] does not have a close feeling to later descendants...When older, they may be punished for their fathers' sins only when they continue perpetrating those sins...and only in the case of idolatry. Concerning other sins, even if the son continues his father's evil ways he will only be punished for his own sins.

V. Individual Accountability

In Ezekiel 18, the prophet resoundingly proclaimed in Hashem's name the principle of individual accountability. People in Israel used to quote a proverb in reference to the punishment of sons for the sins of their fathers: "Parents eat sour grapes and their sons' teeth are blunted" (Ezek. 18:2). A short time prior to Ezekiel, God told Jeremiah (Jer. 31:28) – amid a series of consoling prophecies – that days are coming when this proverb will no longer be cited. Rather, each man will die in his own sin – he who eats the sour grapes, his teeth only will be blunted. It appears that at that point in the history of Israel it was not yet recognized to be the operative principle in theodicy, but there was an assertion of divine acknowledgement that a transition was in formation.

Ezekiel states in Hashem's name:

> What is with you that you quote this proverb upon the soil of Israel, "The fathers eat sour grapes and the

> teeth of their sons are set on edge"? As I live, says the Lord Hashem, you shall no longer quote this proverb in Israel. Behold, all persons are Mine; as the person of the father, so the person of the son, [both] belong to Me; The person who sins, only he shall die…a son who has seen all the sins that his father committed but has considered and not done like them…he shall not die for the iniquity of his father, but shall surely live…and now you ask, "How is it that the son did not bear the iniquity of his father?" The son did what is just and right, he guarded all My statutes and fulfilled them, he shall surely live. The person who sins, he alone shall die. The son shall not bear the iniquity of the father, nor shall the father bear the iniquity of the son; the righteousness of the righteous man shall be accounted to him, and the wickedness of the wicked man shall be accounted to him…
>
> And if the wicked man turns back from the wickedness that he practiced, and guards My statutes and does what is just and right, he shall surely live, not die. All the transgressions that he committed will not be accounted to him; in his righteousness that he has performed he shall live…
>
> Assuredly, O House of Israel, I shall judge each of you according to his ways…Cast off all your transgressions by which you have offended, and make for yourselves a new heart and a new spirit, for why should you die, O House of Israel? For I do not desire that anyone shall die…Repent and live. (Ezek. 18:2-32)

This proclamation, which explicitly states that the righteous son will not share in the punishment of his wicked father, contradicts the biblical clause of "visits the iniquity of fathers upon sons," if the latter is taken without qualification.

In the Talmud (*b. Mak.* 24a), this contradiction is addressed in another manner: "Rabbi Jose the son of Haninah said: Four decrees Moses our master decreed upon Israel – four prophets came and annulled them…Moses said, 'visits the iniquity of fathers upon sons' – Ezekiel came and annulled it, 'the person who sins – only he shall die.'"

In Ezekiel's days Israel's situation had greatly deteriorated and was extremely bleak; indeed, the nation's very survival was in doubt. Whether this prophecy of Ezekiel was proclaimed after the Temple's destruction and the nation's dispersal or shortly before – after the exile of Jehoiachin together with the leaders, eleven years earlier – is not easily resolved, but in any case the people were in deep despair. They felt doomed by their fathers' sins and were beginning to give up all hope in a restoration. It was becoming impossible to maintain their commitment to the covenant without a modification on this critical point. The prophet empathized with their problem and represented their situation to God.

Rabbi Jose the son of Hanina's choice of words – that Moses decreed and Ezekiel annulled – is most unusual. This is a theological matter of the highest order, describing God's mode of governance in the world! Why does he term it Moses' decree? How can we understand this degree of relativity in God's governance?

When asked about such matters, Rabbi Solomon D. Sassoon commented along the following lines. Genuine prophets, fully dedicated to God's will, play a crucial role in matters of the world that fall into their sphere. Their input possesses cosmic significance. Their monumental efforts kept the covenant extant. God considers the prophets' comprehension of His mode of governance crucial to His decision-making and He may modify His methods according to their judgment. God taught this lesson to Abraham upon the latter's exemplifying his extraordinary care for strangers in need and in his obvious commitment to instill *derekh Hashem* ("the way of God") into the world through his descendants and followers. God asked: "Am I to conceal from Abraham that which I am doing?" (Gen. 18:17). He then revealed to Abraham His plans concerning the destruction of Sodom. In the ensuing dialogue that He had with Abraham, He was receptive to the arguments of His faithful servant. A faithful servant of God, who works with total dedication to promote God's will, must have, and indeed is granted, a full measure of personal integrity. Abraham expected a standard of divine providence that human reason may sincerely embrace and Hashem agreed with him.

Life, humanity and society are complex and dynamic. The prophets' conceptions as to what is "just and appropriate" in God's relationship to the world may change from time to time, based on their sincere, ego-less, position and the new circumstances and standards of society. Rabbi Jose the son of Hanina teaches that God is ever sensitive to His faithful servants' honest conceptions and takes their views – which to a certain extent represent the thinking of the righteous and just elements of their constituencies – into account in His governance of the world.

"Zakhor" and "Shamor" Were Uttered As One Word[1]

Rav Yoel Bin-Nun

I. The Reasons for Shabbat in the Ten Commandments in Sefer Shemot and in Sefer Devarim

In comparing the language of the Ten Commandments as they appear in Sefer Shemot and as they appear in Sefer Devarim, we find only a few slight differences, except for the mitzvah of Shabbat where the differences are very clear. The principal difference is not the introductory word – "shamor" or "zakhor" (despite the fact that we interpret "zakhor" as referring to the positive mitzvot of Shabbat, and "shamor" as indicating that we should be careful not to transgress the negative mitzvot) – since the clause 'to keep it holy' is the same in both cases, as is the prohibition to perform "any melakha". The main difference lies rather in the reasons presented for the mitzvah of Shabbat. In each case the reason is stated absolutely, as though it represents the sole basis for the holiness of Shabbat and its prohibitions. In Sefer Shemot the source and reason for Shabbat are in the context of the Creation, while in Sefer Devarim the mitzvah commemorates the exodus from Egypt. The presence of two exclusive reasons would seem to contradict common sense; moreover, it is patently impossible for them to be recited simultaneously, as Chazal explained, except of course by the Holy One, Blessed be He, in a Divine utterance.

---

[1] This article originally appeared in Hebrew, in Megadim Vol. 9, pp. 15-26. It is available online at www.vbm-torah.org/parsha/44vaetch.htm. Translated by Kaeren Fish.

Shemot: You shall perform no melakha, you, your son and your daughter, your man- and maid-servant, and your beast, and the stranger in your gates; For six days God made the heavens and the earth, the sea and all that is in it, and He rested on the seventh day. Therefore, God blessed the Shabbat day and sanctified it.

Devarim: You shall perform no melakha, you, your son and your daughter, your man- and maid-servant, and *your ox and your donkey and all you beasts,* and the stranger in your gates; *in order that your man- and maid-servant rest like you.* And you shall remember that you were a servant in Egypt, and Hashem your God took you out of there with a strong hand and an outstretched arm. Therefore, Hashem your God has commanded you to keep the Shabbat day.

The reason for Shabbat provided in Sefer Shemot presents God as Creator of the Universe, and those who remember and sanctify Shabbat as servants standing before God - as a created person stands before the Creator of all, himself included. Shabbat testifies to the works of Creation, and is an expression of the negation of a person's will, needs and aspirations in the face of the absolute will of the Creator which is revealed in His creation and in the weekly framework of time. Creation *ex nihilo* had no cause; it was not the result of any phenomenon or event, power or law. It was itself the event and the law. Shabbat itself is also an arbitrary timeframe; it is not the result of any natural phenomenon, any other time-related calculation, power or event. The absolute will of the Creator is that one should rest on the seventh day, just as it was His will to create and to perform during the six preceding days. A person who observes Shabbat testifies thereby to the fact that he knows his limitations as a creature, before the Creator of the world. This is a religious perception which is especially revealed among Am Yisrael, although it is not limited to Israel alone. In essence it can also express itself in a natural-universal religion which believes in a God who created the world and man (a possibility raised by Rabbi Yehudah Ha-Levi in his Kuzari, part 1, 11-13), and as it is indeed expressed in religions which drew their inspiration from Judaism (with well-known changes and adjustments).

The reason presented in Sefer Devarim presents God as the Redeemer and Savior of Israel, He Who brought the nation out of Egypt to eternal freedom. Those who observe and sanctify Shabbat stand before God as a free Israelite stands before the Master and Ruler of the world Who breaks the yoke of servitude imposed by human dictators - those kings of flesh and blood who presume in their pagan pride to assume themselves masters of the world. Shabbat bears testimony to the exodus from Egypt, and to freedom in general. It is the flame of freedom borne by the redeemed Israel (and, in fact, anyone redeemed) who can thereafter stand before God, Lord of Israel, as a free nation and accept upon itself Torah and mitzvot.

The prohibitions of *melakhah* on Shabbat here are testimony to human freedom and equality, which came about at the time of the redemption from Egyptian slavery. A person is forbidden to enslave himself, his household members, his workers and servants or the stranger within his gates; even his ox, his donkey and his other beasts are deserving of rest. An Israelite who observes Shabbat testifies thereby to his limitations as a free man - he is forbidden to enslave himself or others. This is a special socio-moral perception. Am Yisrael has a special obligation to observe Shabbat in light of our record of more enslavement and greater redemption than any other nation throughout history. The mitzvah of Shabbat is a central pillar of the Torah which was given to Israel and whose values and principles are dispersed throughout the world by the power of Israel.

Is it really possible for these two concepts to be sounded simultaneously – even when each of them is an absolute justification: "Therefore God blessed.../Therefore God commanded..."? (See Moreh Nevukhim, II:31.)

We have no choice but to return to the formula of Chazal mentioned in the title, which uniquely succeeds in rising above the obvious contradiction and sees the two reasons as two sides of one coin. Each side appears and sounds to many people as representing the entire story, leaving no room for the other. Various groups build their philosophy on one of these two perceptions. The supreme sanctity of the Divine Torah rests precisely on this: that these two perceptions (each complete and absolute as it may be) are simply two sides of the same coin. Only man is unable to comprehend both sides simultaneously! But the Divine utterance included both "zakhor" and "shamor" – both the Creation and the exodus; both "metaphysical religiosity" and "social morality" – at once.

II. Reasons for Shabbat in Sefer Shemot

Actually, both these perceptions of Shabbat have appeared in Sefer Shemot itself, where the reasons for Shabbat are repeated six times, in four distinct groups: In Eilim in the wilderness of Sin, at the time when the manna fell (16); in the ten commandments (20); at the end of Parashat Mishpatim (23:12) and in the parallel renewal of the covenant following the sin of the golden calf (34:21); at the conclusion of the commands regarding the building of the mishkan (31:12-17); and again as the construction of the mishkan gets underway (35:1-3). A detailed comparison of the Shabbat commands in Sefer Shemot (looking first at Eilim [16] and the Ten Commandments [20], and then at

Mishpatim/Ki Tisa [23:12, 34:21] and the two accounts concerning the building of the mishkan [31:12-17, 35:1-3]) reveals the following picture:

	Eilim	Ten Commandments
The Crux of Shabbat	Shabbat for **Israel**; idea of Shabbat already known.	Shabbat already known.
The purpose	Rest: "Rest every man in his place".	Shabbat unto God.
Prohibitions and Commands	Preparation from Friday; two helpings of manna.	Prohibition of all melakha - profane work.
Detail of Prohibitions	Prohibition of household work - baking, cooking - from Friday; prohibition of gathering and going out.	Prohibition is on every Israelite and on all those subject to his authority.
Source and Reason	Exodus from Egypt and manna in the desert (Divine Providence)	Creation (absolute reason)
Punishment	No punishment mentioned but God tests the nation regarding both the manna and Shabbat.	None mentioned.

	Mishpatim/Ki Tisa	Mishkan
The Crux of Shabbat	Positive commandment: you shall rest.	Holy to Israel and holy to God, "shabbat shabbaton"
The purpose	"In order that your ox and donkey will rest and that the son of your maidservant and the stranger will be refreshed."	Significance: eternal covenant, a sign forever between God and Israel, absolute sanctity (overrides even the building of the mishkan).
Prohibitions and Commands	Rest from all work of the field ("You shall rest from plowing and harvesting", "Your work" - "that which you sow in the field")	Absolute prohibition of all melakha, including for the sake of heaven (mishkan). Special prohibition of fire as example of prohibited melakha which is easy to do.
Source and Reason	Exodus from Egypt, from slavery to freedom (23:9,15)	Creation
Punishment	No punishment mentioned.	"karet" and death penalty.

It is clear that the perception of Shabbat in Sefer Devarim already exists in Sefer Shemot, at the end of parashat Mishpatim, as proved by the expression "in order that your ox and donkey will rest." It is equally clear that the reason and command regarding Shabbat are based on a two-fold source – the Creation and the exodus, which appear alternately: at Eilim, in the parasha of the manna, Shabbat is connected with the exodus, while in the Ten Commandments it is connected to the Creation. At the end of Mishpatim we return to the concept of the exodus, and the conclusion of the command regarding the mishkan once again makes mention of the Creation; at the end of Ki Tisa we find the exodus again, and at the beginning of parashat Vayak'hel we return to the Creation.

In the parasha of the manna Shabbat is bound up with the concept of miracle and Divine test:

> And God said to Moshe, "Behold I shall rain down bread for you from the sky, and the nation shall go out and gather daily each day's portion, in order that I may test them to see whether they will walk in the ways of My Torah or not. And it shall be on the sixth day and they shall prepare that which they bring, and it shall be double that which they gather each day." (Shemot 16:4-5).

The test here refers to the actual descent of the manna and to the prohibition of leaving any over until morning [as a test of faith] (16:19-20), as well as to the gathering of a double portion on Friday, and the command not to go out to gather on Shabbat. All of these are bound up with mutual tests: God tests the nation with the waters of Mara ("There He made them a law and a judgment and there He tested them" - Shemot 15:25), and Israel tests God at Refidim ("And he called the place Massa u-meriva for the argument [riv] of the children of Israel and for their testing of God saying, Is God among us or not?" - 17:7).

God's commands here have, aside from the idea of a test, the promise of reward, as we read at the conclusion of the "law and judgment and test" at Mara:

> And He said, "If you will indeed listen to the voice of the Lord your God, and do what is upright in His eyes and hearken to His commandments and observe all His statutes, all the illness which I placed on Egypt I shall not place upon you, for I am the Lord your Healer." (16:26)

In Sefer Devarim, too, the manna is explained in a general sense as a test: “In order to humble you and to test you, to know what was in your hearts, whether you would keep His commandments or not. And He humbled you and made you hungry, and He fed you the manna which you had not known and which your fathers had not known, in order to tell you that man does not live on bread alone; man lives rather on everything that comes forth from God's mouth” (Devarim 8:2-3, 16). The mitzvot of Shabbat appear here as part of the difficult task of addressing questions of faith in Divine Providence and of religious consciousness. The absolute command of Shabbat, devoid of any connection to being tested, to Providence or to reward and punishment actually appears only in the Ten Commandments, and then again while the mishkan is being built.

In the first understanding of Shabbat in the parasha of the manna, **household** melakha is prohibited (Shemot 16), and in the second understanding in parashat Mishpatim we find the prohibition of melakha in the **fields**, which is usually the domain of various types of laborers. In both cases we have principally a positive mitzvah, out of which the various prohibitions arise. The second understanding, at the end of parashat Mishpatim, stands at the root of the Ten Commandments in Sefer Devarim. The mitzvot of Shabbat in the parasha of the manna are connected to the home, not to work in the fields, because the manna represents the very opposite of the produce of the field (“bread from the sky” [Tehillim 105:40]). The only aspect of the manna which involves the outside of the home at all is the gathering and bringing it in - in other words, transferring from one domain to the other. The rest of the melakhot mentioned in connection with manna concern preparation, baking and cooking.

In contrast, the mitzvot of Shabbat at the end of parashat Mishpatim are concerned principally with the field, where the laborers and animals - “your ox and your donkey, the son of your maidservant and the stranger” - are usually to be found. The same idea arises from two comparisons in the same chapter: “And six years shall you sow your land...” (23:10) in contrast to “Six days shall you perform your work...” (23:12), as well as “Six days shall you perform your work...” (ibid.) in contrast to “...and the festival of the ingathering at the end of the year, when you collect your work from the field” (23:16).

We find the same idea in comparing this parasha to the corresponding parasha in Ki Tisa: “Six days shall you do your work, and on the seventh day you shall rest, in order that your ox and your donkey will rest and that the son of your maidservant and the stranger may be refreshed” (23:12), “Six days shall you work, and on the seventh day you shall rest, in the plowing and the harvesting shall you rest” (34:21).

It arises from the above that there are two commands concerning the mitzvah of Shabbat as a positive commandment: Resting at home - prior to the receiving of the Torah, and resting in the field - thereafter. In the Ten Commandments given at Har Sinai the Torah includes “all melakha”, with no distinction, and an absolute prohibition, “lo ta’aseh”, applies to all types of melakha.

The perception of Shabbat against the backdrop of the Creation also has two aspects in Sefer Shemot: In the Ten Commandments we find an absolute prohibition of all “melekhet chol” (profane work), while in the command concerning the mishkan there is an absolute prohibition of all melakha whatsoever, including melakha performed for the sake of Heaven (such as the construction of the mishkan). It is only the second aspect which determines the absolute sanctity of Shabbat, a shabbat-shabbaton which overrides any type of melakha, and "anyone who desecrates it shall surely die." Therefore the punishment for desecrating Shabbat appears only in the parshiot of the mishkan.

III. The Innovation of Sefer Devarim Concerning the Reasons for Shabbat

In light of the connection which we have found between Shabbat at the end of Mishpatim and in the Ten Commandments in Devarim, we are faced with the question of what, if anything, is new and different about the latter rendition.

It seems that the innovation is to be found in three principal areas: firstly, at the end of Mishpatim (Shemot 23:14) there is no "*lo ta'aseh*" (negative command). In Sefer Shemot, the exodus from Egypt gives rise to the obligation of a Shabbat of rest for laborers in the field as a positive commandment, but without any corresponding negative command, since an absolute prohibition arises only from the idea of the Creation. In Devarim the source of the command as arising from the exodus is connected to the absolute prohibition of "You shall do no melakha..."

Secondly, the word "like you" defines the rest which comes with freedom from subjugation to labor on Shabbat on the basis of the equality of worth of all humanity, which goes beyond individual status or the value of any labor. For this reason, in Sefer Devarim the ox and the donkey are separated from the stranger and the maidservant and are inserted in their proper place, immediately prior to "and all your beasts."

> <u>Shemot</u> (23 and 34): Six days shall you perform your work (in chapter 34, "shall you work") (in the field) and on the seventh day you shall rest, in order that your ox and donkey may rest (physical rest) and that

the son of your maidservant and the stranger shall be refreshed (*veyinafesh* -physical rest).

Devarim (5): Six days shall you work and perform all your melakha, and the seventh day is a Shabbat unto the Lord your God; you shall not perform any melakha - you, your son and your daughter, your man- and maidservant, and your ox and your donkey and all your beasts, and the stranger who is within your gates - in order that your manservant and maidservant will rest like you.

Freedom and rest are arranged from the bottom upwards according to the various hierarchical positions enumerated at the end of Mishpatim: animals first and then man; servant and then stranger - like the hierarchy which exists in a large portion of the mishpatim (social laws) themselves. (See principally chapter 21 from verse 12 in decreasing status: man-servant-embryo-animal.) In Sefer Devarim there is a change: the ox and the donkey are not to perform any melakha, as part of the all-encompassing prohibition, but the manservant and maidservant and the stranger are to rest "like you".

The third – and most important – innovation of Sefer Devarim is that the presentation of the exodus as the source for the commandment of Shabbat becomes generalized and absolute: "Therefore the Lord your God commanded you to observe the day of Shabbat."

IV. Summary

It is specifically Sefer Devarim which places Shabbat absolutely against the backdrop of the exodus as the source of freedom and the equality of Bnei Yisrael before their God Who brought them from slavery to eternal freedom.

The ideals of freedom and equality which have become so popular in our generation are based, without any doubt, on the exodus, and they are written in the Divine Torah given to Israel by Moshe's hand - especially in Sefer Devarim. (It is only idolatry and its attendant phenomena which are given no freedom or leeway in Sefer Devarim - since true freedom comes only from God!)

Haftarah of Shabu`ot's Second Day (Habaquq 2:20-3:19)

Rabbi Ralph Tawil

A *baraita* in the Babylonian Talmud (*Megilla* 31a) that describes all the special readings and haftarot of the year states:

> On Shabu`ot (*`Asseret*) [we read] "Seven weeks..." (Deuteronomy 15:9) and we conclude with "Habaquq." Others say [that we read] "On the third month" (Exodus 19:1) and conclude with "the chariot" (Ezekiel 1.) Now that we have two days, we practice like both.

Rashi, explaining the custom to read Habaquq, says:

> Since [Habaquq] speaks about the giving of the Torah, [as in the verse] "God is coming from Teman"– at the giving of the Torah.

Since Shabu`ot is the festival on which we celebrate the revelation at Mount Sinai, which happened in this time of the year, this haftarah reflects the experience of God's revealing Himself to man. (Actually, both haftarot of this holiday focus more upon the prophetic experience of God's revelation.)

Since this is the only time of the year when Habaquq is read as a Haftarah (for those living outside of Israel) we will give some background about Habaquq and the book that bears his name. Who was Habaquq? When did he live? What are the major concepts and characteristics of his prophecy?

As is common for many of the "later" prophets, especially those whose literary legacy was small (the "twelve prophets") we know very little about the biography of Habaquq. The only clue we have about the time of his prophecy is one word in the first chapter that identifies the enemy nation that will come to plunder Israel – the *Kasdim* (Chaldeans):

> Look among the nations, observe well and be utterly astounded; for a work is being wrought in your days which you would not believe if it were told. For lo, I am raising up the Chaldeans, that fierce and impetuous nation, who cross the earth's wide spaces to seize homes not their own. They are terrible, dreadful; they make their own laws and rules. Their horses are swifter than leopards, fleeter than wolves of the steppe. Their steeds gallop – their steeds come flying from afar. Like vultures rushing toward food, they all come, bent on rapine. (1:5-8)

From these verses, it is clear that this *Kasdim* empire is on the ascendancy. This most likely places the prophecy at the last third of the 7th century BCE – at the beginning of the Neo-Babylonian Empire.

Another factor that points towards this period is that Habaquq tends to paraphrase extensively from other prophetic works. These works include Micha, Yeshaya, and Yirmiya. For example, compare the description of the Babylonians above with Yirmiya's description:

> Lo, he ascends like clouds, his chariots are like a whirlwind, his horses are swifter than eagles. Woe to us we are ruined. (Jer. 4:13)

Many paraphrases like this one imply dependence between Habaquq and these prophets. However, the prophets that Habaquq paraphrases are only those who prophesied before the end of the seventh century BCE. They do not include later prophets. This supports the dating of Habaquq to that period. Hazal also date Habaquq to the reign of Menashe (696-641), which is very close to the proposed dating.[1]

The book that contains Habaquq's prophecy is three chapters long. These chapters could be divided into two sections consisting of (a) chapters 1-2 and (b) chapter 3 (the haftarah). The first chapter consists of a question posed by the prophet to God upon foreseeing the rise of the cruel Babylonians. The question is that of theodicy:

> You whose eyes are too pure to look upon evil, Who cannot countenance wrongdoing, why do You countenance treachery, and stand by idle while the one in the wrong devours the one in the right? (1:13)

The second chapter begins with a daring statement by Habaquq who threatens:

> I will stand on my watch, take up my station at the post, and wait to see what He will say to me, what He will reply to my complaint. (2:1)

God meets the challenge and responds using both logical argument (*qal vaḥomer*) and parable:

> Lo, his spirit within him is puffed up, not upright, but the righteous man is rewarded with life for his fidelity. How much less then shall the defiant go unpunished, the treacherous, arrogant man who has made his maw as wide as Sheol, who is as insatiable as Death, who has harvested all the nations and gathered in all the peoples. (2:4-5 [NJPS])

---

[1] Yoel, Nahhum and Habaquq prophesied in the days of Menashe. Since he (Menashe) was not "kosher" they were not mentioned together with his name. As it is said: "And God spoke to Menashe and to his people and they did not listen" (2 Chronicles 33:10). (*Seder Olam Rabbah* 20)

God's answer is that these wicked people will eventually suffer a bitter end and be punished severely by God. God introduces His answer that even if the retribution of the wicked "tarries, wait for it still."

Five short sections follow this answer. The first four containing parables said by the captured nations assuring the downfall of their captor. The last section contrasts the dumb idols with the All-powerful God:

> What has the carved image availed, that he who fashioned it has carved it for an image and a false oracle – that he who fashioned his product has trusted in it, making dumb idols? Ah, you who say, "Wake up" to wood, "Waken" to inert stone! Can that give an oracle? Why, it is encased in gold and silver, but there is not breath inside it. But the Lord in His holy abode – be silent before Him all the earth. (2:18-20)

The custom of most communities, except the Italian Jewish community, is to begin the haftarah from the last verse of Habaquq chapter 2:20 (quoted above). The Italian community begins directly with chapter 3. Although, it makes more sense to begin with chapter 3 as that is clearly a different, self-contained chapter, the end of chapter 2, presents a concept which is important concerning the context of the reading, the day commemorating the revelation at Sinai, where God, in all His might, revealed Himself to His people.

Chapter 3 begins with the prophet's prayer to God not to delay His coming. The prophet prays:

> O Lord! I have learned of Your renown; I am awed, O Lord, by Your deeds. Renew them in these years, Oh, make them known in these years! Though angry, may You remember compassion. (3:2)

In chapter 2 God had answered Habaquq's question by saying that eventually the wicked nation will suffer. Habaquq responds in chapter 3 with a prayer that God expedite the punishment of the wicked.

The next section contains the prophecy that describes what the world would experience when God appears. These verses are the reason for the choice of this section as the Haftarah for Shabu`ot's second day:

> God is coming from Teman, the Holy one from mount Paran. His majesty covers the skies, His splendor fills the earth: It is a brilliant light which gives off rays one every side – and therein His glory is enveloped. Pestilence marches before Him, and plague comes forth at His heels. When He stands, He measures the earth, when He glances He makes nations tremble. The age-old mountains are shattered, the primeval hills sink low. (3:3-6)

As in the earlier chapters of Habaquq, this chapter is filled with quotations from other sources. For example, notice the similarity of the beginning of these verses describing God's appearance with the song of Moshe:

> The Lord came from Sinai; He shone upon them from Seir; He appeared from Mount Paran, and approached from Ribeboth-kodesh. Lightening flashing at His right. (Deuteronomy 33:2).

The straightforward understanding of these verses in the context of the book of Habaquq is that this revelation is not one that happened in the past (as the verses of Deuteronomy 33 imply) but a revelation in the future. This future revelation will be of similar proportions as the revelations of God in the past; of similar earth-shattering proportions, but of different purpose.

Habaquq is clear about the purpose of the God's future revelation:

> The mountains rock at the sight of You, a torrent of rain comes down; Loud roars the deep, the sky returns the echo. Sun and moon stand still on high as Your arrows fly in brightness, Your flashing spears in brilliance. You tread the earth in rage, You trample nations in fury.
>
> You have come forth to deliver Your people, to deliver Your anointed. You will smash the roof of the villain's house, raze it from foundation to top. You will crack his skull with Your bludgeon; blown away shall be his warriors, whose delight is to crush me suddenly, to devour a poor man in ambush. (3:10-14)

The future revelation is not to receive a Torah, but to destroy Israel's enemies.

The book ends with the prophet reacting joyfully to the envisioned appearance of God and the inevitable triumph over Israel's enemies.

In summary, the prophet Habaquq foresees the rise of the evil nation Babel who will plunder and destroy Israel. He complains to God about the injustice of this wicked nation defeating the righteous Israel. God responds that eventually this nation will be punished. Habaquq is not satisfied with this eventuality and prays that the destruction come sooner. He envisions how God's appearance and the eventual destruction of Israel's enemies would unfold and is filled with joy and trust in God.

Wilderness and Revelation[1]

Rabbi Lord Jonathan Sacks

The sedra [parashah] of Bemidbar – "In the wilderness" – is usually (though not this year) read directly before the festival of Shavuot, "the time of the giving of the Torah," when we recall the revelation at Mount Sinai. Indeed the opening verse refers to Sinai: "And the Lord spoke to Moses in the wilderness of Sinai…" What is the connection between wilderness and revelation?

The Midrash makes a psychological spiritual point: Anyone who does not make himself open to all [*hefker*, literally ownerless] like a wilderness cannot acquire wisdom and Torah (Bemidbar Rabbah 1:7). The desert is neither public nor private space. It belongs to no one. It is completely exposed to the sun and the elements. So must we be – imply the sages – if we are to become the recipients of Torah. To hear its commanding voice we must listen with total openness, absolute humility. Torah speaks to the soul that has learnt the art of silence.

The Egyptian-French poet Edmond Jabès (1912-1991) noted the connection between *d-b-r*, 'word,' and *m-d-b-r*, 'wilderness.' For him, the wilderness experience is an essential and continuing feature of what it is to be a Jew:

> With exemplary regularity the Jew chooses to set out for the desert, to go toward a renewed word that has become his origin…A wandering word is the word of God. It has for its echo the word of a wandering people. No oasis for it, no shadow, no peace. Only the

[1] The following article was taken from Rabbi Lord Jonathan Sacks' weekly parasha studies *Covenant and Conversation* for Parashat Bemidbar (5769), available online at www.rabbisacks.org.

> immense, thirsty desert, only the book of this thirst... (*From the Book to the Book,* pp. 166-67)

For Jabès, the desert – with its unearthly silence and emptiness – is the condition in which the Word can be heard. There, between sand and sky, the unmediated encounter takes place between God and His people. There is something stark and austere about the wilderness, as there is about Judaism. In no other religion do God and humanity stand in such direct closeness, engaging in such frank and direct dialogue. Judaism is faith stripped of all accretions of myth – a faith that could only reach its full expression far from the diversions and distractions of urban or rural culture, in a landscape of lonely figures confronting the immensity of nature and hearing the Word from above and beyond. We are, Jabès implies, a desert people, never fully at home, never altogether satisfied, always thirsting for something that eludes us, never feeling that we have yet reached our destination. Judaism is the-word-as-wilderness and the-wilderness-as-word.

For the prophets, the desert signaled something else – privacy, intimacy, a place where Lover and beloved go to be alone with one another. Jeremiah delivers one of the most beautiful lines in the entire prophetic literature. In striking contrast to the impression we receive elsewhere in Tanakh, that the Israelites in the wilderness were quarrelsome and rebellious, Jeremiah speaks of the love and trust of the people, willing to leave all they knew and follow the divine call:

> I remember the devotion of your youth, your love as a bride – how you followed Me in the wilderness, in a land not sown. (Jeremiah 2:1)

In an earlier age, Hosea used the wilderness as a symbol of the betrothal between God and the Israelites. God had 'married' the people, but they had acted unfaithfully. God would punish them. They would suffer disasters. Yet he could not abandon them, so great was His love. So, in an act of reconciliation, he would bring them back and renew their marriage vows in the wilderness, understood as a kind of second honeymoon:

> Therefore I am now going to allure her; I will lead her into the wilderness and speak tenderly to her. There I will give her back her vineyards, and will make the Valley of Achor a door of hope. There she will sing as in the days of her youth, as in the day she came up out of Egypt. (Hosea 2:16-17)

But there is a further, immensely significant dimension to the fact that the Torah was given in the wilderness. Israel, alone among the nations of world history, received its constitution even before it had entered its land. There is no analogy to this anywhere else. For every other nation, the land long preceded the laws. A people live in a certain territory. Gradually they begin to associate in ever larger groupings. They fight wars, build settlements, adopt leaders, develop a political structure, and then create a body of legislation to regulate their affairs. Nations develop organically like plants, with their roots in a soil, a landscape. In the history of Israel, and nowhere else, the nation received its laws in the wilderness, before it had even seen, let alone settled, the land. This is one of the great paradoxes of Judaism.

On the one hand, the Jewish story is about the land of Israel. It begins with Abraham's journey toward it. It continues with a second journey in the days of Moses, with the family now become a people. Judaism is a religion of place: the holy land, the physical location in which the people of the covenant are summoned to create a sacred society based on justice and compassion, human dignity and freedom. It was to be stand in the greatest possible contrast to the great empires with which it was surrounded–nations predicated on demographic strength and military power, tyrannical regimes and hierarchical societies with absolute rulers and populations measured in the mass, not the worth of the individual. Judaism has a home, a place where it belongs.

Yet most of Jewish history was spent outside that home. Abraham was forced, by famine, into exile. So was Jacob. Genesis ends with the patriarchal family in Egypt. Deuteronomy ends with Moses in sight of the promised land but not destined to enter it. Jewish history is a story of exiles – to Assyria, then Babylon, then the long series of dispersions from the Roman conquest to the birth of the modern State of Israel in 1948. As Isaiah Berlin noted:

> It was once said by the celebrated Russian revolutionary, Alexander Herzen, writing in the mid-nineteenth century, that the Slavs had no history, only geography. The position of the Jews is the reverse of this. They have enjoyed rather too much history and too little geography. (*The Power of Ideas*, p. 143)

This paradox is essential to Judaism and what makes it unique among the world's faiths. On the one hand, the God of Israel is utterly unlike the gods of the ancient world. He is not confined to this place, that nation: He is everywhere. Yet He is not remote, abstract. He has a home – or, to put it more precisely, He lives among a people that has a home. That is why Judaism is attached to a holy land – but at the same time it remains God's people even when in exile from the land.

It is thus no accident that the Israelites received their greatest revelation – the moment that forged them into a nation – outside the land, Bemidbar, 'in the wilderness', the place that is not a place, just as Jacob received his two great revelations (the vision of a ladder stretching from earth to heaven, and the wrestling match with a stranger) in the midst of journeys, in places that were between: neither starting point nor destination.

The giving of the Torah in the wilderness is an essential feature of Jewish history. Had the Israelites received the Torah in the land, it would be indissolubly associated with the land. Exile would mean the end of the covenant. It would make no more sense to keep Torah while in exile than to obey the laws of Russia while living in Spain. What made the God of Israel different was the fact that He was sovereign of the universe, not a local deity. That is why the Jewish people survived dispersion. Only the God of everywhere can be found and worshipped anywhere.

Shavuot, Revelation and Learning[1]

Rabbi Nathan Lopes Cardozo

In Pirke Avot (Ethics of the Fathers) 3:10, we find a rather exorbitant statement by one of the Sages:

> Rabbi Dostai ben Yanai said in the name of Rabbi Meir: "Whoever forgets even one thing of his Torah learning, Scripture regards him as though he is guilty to pay with his life, for it is said: 'Be careful and guard your life greatly, lest you forget the things you saw (at the time of the revelation at Sinai) with your own eyes, and lest they be removed from your heart your entire lifetime, and you shall inform your children and grandchildren of them, the day you stood before God, your God at Chorev…'" (Devarim 4:9-10)

Why should the failure to remember a part of Torah which one learned give evidence to the fact that one forgot that what one had seen with his own eyes when he stood at Sinai? Besides the fact that forgetfulness is a normal human condition, there is also a great difference between the power of sight and the act of learning. In the case of the generation which actually stood at Sinai, we understand why such people should be liable. They actually saw the revelation at Sinai. But why should those who did not stand at Sinai and "only" learned Torah and afterwards forgot, be liable as well? How could Rabbi Dostai compare anybody who lives thousands of years after the revelation with those who actually stood at Sinai?

In his commentary on the Torah, Ramban states that the verse quoted above clearly focuses on the circumstances

[1] The following article is available online at cardozoacademy.org/holidays/shavuot/shavuot-revelation-and-learning-ttp-18.

under which the Torah was given and not on the actual contents of the Torah. In that case, it is even more difficult to see how the observation by Rabbi Dostai is borne out by the verse he quotes as his proof. He points to the fact that those who learn the contents of the Torah and then forget what they learned are guilty to pay with their lives, but his proof is derived from a statement which speaks about the need to keep the circumstances under which the Torah was given and not about its content.

It is rather interesting to note that the Sinai experience never gave rise to a special day in the Jewish calendar. Although it is true that Shavuot is traditionally seen as the day of the giving of the Torah, it is still remarkable that there is no such connection made in the biblical text – it was the Sages who made this connection. Shavuot mainly appears as a festival celebrating the new harvest (see Vayikra 23:9-22). Neither does the Torah command the Israelites to observe a special mitzvah with the purpose to reenact this unique moment in Jewish history. Compare this to the case of Pesach or Sukkot. These historical events are translated into numerous mitzvoth such as the consumption of matzah and the dwelling in the Sukkah.

We must, therefore, draw the conclusion that while the festivals like Pesach and Sukkot need to be contemporized every year, there is no such need when dealing with the event of revelation. Pesach and Sukkot celebrate events which took place in the past and through reenacting them by means of such commandments as matzah and sukkah, the Jew is able to experience them once more.

This is not so when we deal with the moment of revelation. There is no need to commemorate the event! We believe the reason for this is most telling. One does not commemorate something which takes place in the "here and now," just as it would be an affront to commemorate a human being when he is living with us is the present day.

By refusing to give the revelation at Sinai any commemoration, the Torah makes the crucial point that the revelation at Sinai is not a past experience which needs to be reactivated in the present (like Pesach or Sukkot). It is an ongoing adventure! At Sinai the revelation started, but it never came to a close. Its words perpetuate and persist. But how does this revelation continue? It continues through the Torah itself, by its study. Learning Torah is revelation! The Torah is not the record of that what once happened at Sinai, but that which takes place now while we study Torah. Granted, it is rooted in the moment of Sinai when it started to penetrate into our universe, but that moment continues to unfold.

As such, learning Torah is neither the study of what happened a long time ago nor what God once commanded man to do. Rather it is the confrontation with the divine word at this present moment. Torah learning is made from completely different components from any other study known to man. It is not a confrontation with a text but with a voice. And it is not just listening to this voice which is required, but it is a type of higher level hearing which comes about through actively responding to that voice. This is accomplished through the careful observance of the commandments. It is the divine voice which is captured and becomes tangible in the fulfillment of the mitzvoth. "One hears differently when one hears in doing," Franz Rosenzweig, the famous philosopher and *baal teshuva* once observed.[2] Said differently, there is an experiential difference between a secular act of reading or studying a text, and the religious act of listening to Torah.

We are now able to understand Rabbi Dostai's observation: One can only forget that which was, but one cannot forget what is. Learning Torah is equivalent to

---

[2] Franz Rosenzweig, *On Jewish Learning* (Schocken, NY: 1955).

standing at Sinai. Learning Torah is seeing its contents handed over at Sinai in the "here and now." So the learning of its text is a religious happening, the experience of that which normally can only be recalled. The moment one forgets Torah, one transgresses "Lest you forget the things which you saw." This could not mean anything else but that when one has reached the point where his Torah knowledge may be forgotten, it must be the result of something which he saw and not what he sees! But when one learns Torah as a religious experience and one sees its revelation alive, then the gap of several thousand years from the time when the revelation started and where it finds itself now no longer exists. As such Torah is given today and Rabbi Dostai draws our attention to a major foundation of Jewish belief.

Mimahorat HaShabbat[1]

Rabbi Yitzchak Etshalom

I. Introduction

In a previous essay, we discussed the textual problem in Vayyikra 23, which was the basis for the most ferocious expression of the Sadducean-Pharisaic schism during the end of the Second Commonwealth:

> And he shall wave the sheaf before Hashem, to be accepted for you; *Mimahorat haShabbat* (on the next day after the Shabbat) the priest shall wave it. And you shall offer that day when you wave the sheaf a male lamb without blemish of the first year for a burnt offering to Hashem…And you shall count *Mimahorat haShabbat*, from the day that you brought the sheaf of the wave offering; seven Sabbaths shall be complete; To *Mimahorat haShabbat haShevi'it* (the next day after the seventh Shabbat) shall you count fifty days; and you shall offer a new meal offering to Hashem. (23:11-12, 15-16)

As outlined in Part I of this study, the Boethusians (an offshoot of the Sadducees), maintained that the Shabbat in the key phrase *Mimahorat haShabbat* refers to the *Shabbat Bereshit* (the weekly Sabbath) and, as such, the Omer offering must always be brought on a Sunday. Consequently, the festival of Shavu'ot would also be, seven weeks later, on a Sunday.

The Pharisaic position was that the Omer offering was to be brought on the day after the Yom Tov of *Hag*

---

[1] This essay is part two of a two part *shiur* on Shavu'ot. It is available online at http://www.torah.org/advanced/mikra/5770/shavuos.html?print=1.

haMatzot (16th of Aviv [Nisan]), regardless of which day of the week that festival occurred.

The Pharisaic/Halakhic position was – and continues to be – argued by *Ba'alei haMesorah*, regardless of the lack of presence of an active proponent of the Boethusian position. Throughout the ages, all *Parshanim* (commentators) addressed the issue, even if there were no "Sunday Shavu'ot" lobbyists in their generation. In this essay we will share a contemporary approach to the problem, one which has never (before now) seen the light of the publishing day. Pursuant to that, I will outline and suggest a novel approach which, hopefully, will be worthy of inclusion in the ever-growing list of proofs of the Rabbinic position as to the date of Shavu'ot.

Before sharing these responses and defenses of the Pharisaic position, it behooves us to delve a bit more deeply into the Boethusian position. In last week's essay, we discussed the textual rationale for their position (and the attendant difficulties, even sans Masoretic opposition). In this essay, we will analyze some of the motivation for their choice of interpretation.

II. The Judean Desert Scrolls

Perhaps the single most significant archeological discovery in the 20th Century (a century marked by dozens of critical finds at digs throughout the Levant) was the Dead Sea Scrolls. The Scrolls, found in a series of caves in the Judean desert, were accidentally unearthed by two young Bedouin shepherds in 1947 who, trying to retrieve a lost goat, happened upon seven nearly complete scrolls encased in clay jars. The ensuing search (by both Bedouins and archeologists) brought to light hundreds of scrolls that had been composed between the fourth century BCE and the first century CE. Over the past fifty years, much scholarly research has been devoted to deciphering these scrolls and comparing them with literature extant at the same time. Over this time, academicians who specialize in "the Scrolls" have attempted to determine, among other facts, the identity of the group that resided in the vicinity of these caves and which was responsible for the composition of the many documents.

Among the documents found are liturgical poems, letters, copies of canonized text from Tanakh as well as books of the Apocrypha and Pseudepigrapha, Midrashic expansions of those books (known as *Pesharim*)—along with codes of practice. These codes not only contain the practices of the Qumran community, but, in some cases, record the polemics of their dispute with the Pharisaic community. A fascinating development of "Scrolls research" has been to "finally" see the mirror image of disputes recorded in Rabbinic literature – from the perspective of the Rabbinates opposite number. For instance, at the end of Mishnah *Yadayim* (4:7), there is a record of a Sadducean complaint against the Pharisees: "We complain against you Pharisees, for you declare pure the *Nitzoq* (poured out liquid stream)." This statement is followed by the counter-argument proffered by the Hakhamim - however, for the roughly 1700 years between the publication of the Mishnah (c. 220 CE) until the publication of the *Mik'tzat Ma'aseh Torah* ("Halakhic Letter"), students of the Mishnah had no access to the Sadducean perspective of this debate. With the discovery and subsequent publication of *Mik'tzat Ma'aseh Torah* we find the following argument put forth:

> And even regarding liquid streams, we say that they do not have purity. And even the liquid streams do not separate between the impure and the pure. For the moisture of the liquid streams and the vessel which receives from them are both considered one identical moisture. (MMT B56-58)

> [The case in question deals with a pure vessel that is the source of a liquid stream which flows into an impure vessel. The Sadducean position was that the water is all one; therefore the upper vessel is rendered impure by the lower vessel. The Rabbinic position is that the lower vessel has no effect on the upper vessel]. (Cf. M. Makh'shirin 5:9, MT Tum'at Okh'lin 7:1)

This find is much more than a historical curiosity of purely academic/research concern; by seeing the "counter-argument" spelled out, we can better identify the group which resided in the desert and authored (or, at least copied and maintained) these scrolls. Whereas earlier indications were that the "Qumran community" was made up of Essenes, the publication of *Mik'tzat Ma'aseh Torah* has provided much support for the theory that these sectarians were Sadducees (or an offshoot of that group) as indicated by the example cited above. This is critical for our purposes, as any information found in the Scrolls can be helpful in helping us understand the Sadducean position - a position with which we were only familiar from Rabbinic sources until now.

Among the many significant passages in the *Mik'tzat Ma'aseh Torah* is the calendar of the community. Although there is much scholarly debate as to whether this calendar was ever put into practice, this solar calendar is quite clearly spelled out and sheds much light on the motivation behind the Boethusian position in the debate regarding the date of the Omer offering and Shavu'ot.

The calendar (taken here from pp. 302-303 of Lawrence Schiffman's "Reclaiming the Dead Sea Scrolls", the source for much of the background information above) consisted of a 364-day year, constituting exactly 52 weeks. Each month had thirty days and, in order to keep the calendar in line with the equinoxes and solstices, a thirty-first day was added to every third month.

As a result of the exact weeks (with no remaining days) in this calendar, each Festival occurred on the same day of the week every year. [It is difficult to imagine how a calendar of this sort could ever be maintained without regular correction for the missing 30 hours every solar year; that is why, as pointed out above, many scholars claim that this calendar was never actually put into practice.] Here are the days found in the Scrolls calendar which have relevance to our discussion:

- *Pesach* (14th of First Month) - Tuesday
- *Matzot* (15th of First Month) - Wednesday
- *Omer*-offering (26th of First Month) - Sunday
- First Fruits of Wheat offering (*Shavu'ot* - 15th of Third Month) - Sunday

There are two points to be noted here:

1) Pesach (the day of the Pesach offering) would always fall on a Tuesday. One contemporary scholar has suggested that this explains the curious passage in BT Pesahim 66a, relating that the Hakhamim did not recall if the Pesach offering should be brought when the fourteenth of Nisan fell on Shabbat [the offering would constitute several violations of Shabbat] until Hillel was consulted. Why wouldn't they remember the Halakhah? After all, under normal circumstances, Pesach should fall on Shabbat every few years - certainly not too long to remember the proper procedure. The suggestion was made that since the Sadducees exercised significant control over the Beit HaMikdash during the first century BCE and into the millennium, their calendar was in operation during those years and, indeed, there had been many years since Pesach

had fallen on Shabbat. To adopt this explanation, we would have to posit that the calendar was actually put to use and not just theoretical.

2) This also explains the curious wording of the Mishnah in *Menahot* (10:4). In explaining the "great fuss" attendant upon the cutting of the *'Omer*'s worth of barley, the Mishnah states that this was done to contradict the Boethusians "who maintained that the cutting of the 'Omer is not done on *Motza'ei Yom Tov* (the night following the Festival)." The claim attributed to the Boethusians is odd; one would have expected them to state: "The cutting of the 'Omer is done on Saturday night" which proves to be the bone of contention as developed in the Talmudic discussion ad loc. Awareness of this calendar explains the wording - it wasn't the case (as most students of the Talmudic passages have assumed) that the Boethusians held that the cutting of the 'Omer must be on a Saturday night; rather, they had a particular date (a few days after the end of *Hag haMatzot*) on which the 'Omer was to be cut (and offered).

In sum, we can now understand several facets of the Boethusian dispute, most notably their motivation for interpreting the key phrase *Mimahorat haShabbat* as a reference to Sunday. Within a calendar system that prizes consistency of days of the week in relation to annual festivals, it is easy to understand why the favored interpretation would render a given festival as occurring on a set day of the week.

III. One Contemporary Solution: Understanding the Role of the "Key Word" And the Hapax Legomenon

In last year's series on Megillat Ruth, we spent some time analyzing the role of the *Milah Manhah* (key word) which helps to guide our appreciation of the underlying theme of the Parashah. We will again turn our attention to the role of the *Milah Manhah* to share a contemporary solution to the problem of *Mimahorat haShabbat*.

There is a not-insignificant number of words which only appear in Tanakh once – such a word is known as a *Milah Yehida'it* (singular word) or *hapax legomenon*. The meaning of such a word is often elusive; if the immediate context is not clear, there is no parallel text to which to turn.

Professor Yehuda Elitzur z"l suggests that there are two different types of occurrences of the *hapax legomenon*, each based on a different motivation of the text:

1) Where the singular word is of a technical nature and there simply is no reason to mention it in any other passage. An example (there are many) of this type is the singular word *Pim* found among the list of farm-implements which the B'nei Yisrae'l had to take down to the *Pelishtim* for honing, since the *Pelishtim* did not allow the B'nei Yisra'el to work as smiths out of fear that they would fashion weapons (I Sh'mu'el 13:19-22). The word *Pim*, being unmatched, was hard for the classical commentators to decipher and they raised a number of intriguing possibilities – which range far and wide and, as it turns out, are not true to the meaning of the text. It was only as a result of archeological digs in Eretz Yisra'el that several coins, bearing the word *Pim* on them, surfaced – clarifying the meaning of the text. In any case, the occurrence of this sort of *hapax legomenon* is readily understandable.

2) When it is clear from context that the word in question is being used in lieu of a more familiar word. An example of this is the word *Avur* (which appears twice, but within the same context and bearing the same meaning, thus still qualifying as a singular word). We noted the

passage in which this word appears in last week's essay (Rambam's proof):

> And the people of Yisra'el encamped in Gilgal, and kept the Pesach on the fourteenth day of the month in the evening in the plains of Yericho. And they ate of the *Avur ha'Aretz* of the land on the next day after the Pesach, unleavened cakes, and parched grain in the same day. (Yehoshua 5:10-11)

The word *Avur*, as indicated by the context, refers to some sort of bounty (either the new grain, as per Rambam, or specifically the old grain, as per Radak). In any case, the text follows this line with a seemingly superfluous phrase:

> And the *Mahn* ceased on the next day after they had eaten of the *Avur ha'Aretz*; nor had the people of Yisra'el *Mahn* anymore; but they ate of the *Tevu'at ha'Aretz* (fruit of the land) of Kena'an that year. (v. 12)

Although news of the cessation of the *Mahn* is necessary, why does the text have to repeat its observation that the people ate of the fruit of the Land from that point on?

Professor Elitzur suggests that since the word *Avur* is not attested to in any other passages and may be misunderstood by the reader, the text is clarifying that what it means is *Tevu'ah* - a much more familiar word. That being the case, why use *Avur* at all?

Here is where our awareness of the *Milah Manhah* comes to bear. The chapters which detail the crossing of the people in the Land (chapters 3-4) have a preponderance of occurrences of the root *'abr* (to pass). Within those two brief chapters and the beginning of Chapter 5, the root shows up, in one form or another, close to 30 times (besides numerous alliterative allusions). In other words, the key word – and underlying theme – of this section of the text is "passing over." Therefore, argues Elitzur, the text utilizes an uncommon word which uses the same root and which means "bounty." The sense is that the entire process of passing over was only completed after they had begun eating of the produce of the Land.

In sum, there are two categories of the singular word – where it is the most appropriate word but there is only one occasion for the text to use it, and where the text deliberately chooses that word in order to link it with the ongoing theme of the text.

Using this theory, Professor Elitzur suggests that the use of *Mahorat haShabbat* in our selection is motivated by much the same considerations. As we pointed out in our earlier discussion of *Parashat haMo'adot* (V'shinantam 3/32), an oft-repeated word in the entire chapter (Vayyikra 23) is Shabbat. Not only is the weekly Shabbat surprisingly included in the list of the festivals, but Yom haZikkaron ("Rosh haShanah"), Yom haKippurim, Sukkot and Sh'mini Atzeret are all described as a "*Shabbaton*."

We are aware of Shabbat exclusively as a description of the weekly "Sabbath" and, by extension, the Sabbatical year. In Akkadian documents, however, there is ample mention of a monthly day of rest that took place on the fifteenth of every month - and which was called *Sappatu*. In other words, although our Shabbat is the weekly day of rest, commemorating (among other things) creation, the word does have an alternate meaning which is older than Sinai – a monthly day of cessation from labor on the full moon. (We need not accept the many fantastic and heretical theories about the "evolution" of Shabbat which arise from this observation to utilize the philological association.) M. Fishbane (Biblical Interpretation in Ancient Israel, pp. 148-151) goes so far as to suggest that the common pairing of *Hodesh* and Shabbat in Tanakh (e.g. II Melakhim 4:23) is a reference to the two monthly "special days," one at the onset of the lunar cycle and the other at its peak. Again, we need not accept this interpretation, fascinating though it may be, in order to allow the ancient meaning of Shabbat/*Sappatu* to shed light on our problem.

Professor Elitzur suggests that since the entire *Parashat haMo'adot* (Vayyikra 23) is themed by the notion of Shabbat (as demonstrated above), the text utilized this word in an unusual and "outdated" meaning (the fifteenth of the month), and inasmuch the same fashion as the book of Yehoshua used *Avur*. In other words, the proper wording here would have been *Mimahorat haHag* – but, since the *Milah Manhah* here is Shabbat, the text used it in lieu of *Hag*, referring to its ancient meaning.[2]

IV. A Final Suggestion: Using Structure to Determine Meaning

We have, in past essays, discussed the literary structure of selections from Tanakh and demonstrated that, at times, the structure itself lends meaning and clarification to the text in question.

There are occasions when, if we can properly determine the structure of a Parashah, that determination will help us decipher enigmatic words or phrases.

The section in which our nettlesome phrase appears constitutes two Parashiot, all of which are one *Dibbur* (speech). A careful perusal of the text reveals a clear and consistent structure, known as a chiasmus. In a chiastic structure the outer ends of the text present parallel or opposite (but matching) ideas, using similar phrases to

---

[2] I am most indebted to my teacher and friend, Dr. Yoel Elitzur, for sharing his father's suggestion with me and allowing me to bring it to print for the first time. I am confident that when he publishes the article, it will be much more persuasive and erudite.

form the connection. Each subsequent verse or phrase matches its partner until the middle - which is the focus of the Parashah. This chiasmus can be schematized as ABCDEFEDCBA:

> **[A]** And Hashem spoke to Moses, saying, Speak to the people of Yisra'el, and say to them, When you come to the land which I give to you, and shall reap its harvest, then you shall bring a sheaf of the first fruits of your harvest to the priest;
>
> **[B]** And he shall wave the sheaf before Hashem, to be accepted for you; *Mimahorat haShabbat* (on the next day after the Shabbat) the priest shall wave it.
>
> **[C]** And you shall offer that day when you wave the sheaf a male lamb without blemish of the first year for a burnt offering to Hashem.
>
> **[D]** And the meal offering of it shall be two tenth deals of fine flour mixed with oil, an offering made by fire to Hashem for a sweet savor; and the drink offering of it shall be of wine, the fourth part of a *hin*.
>
> **[E]** And you shall eat nor bread, nor parched grain, nor green ears, until the same day that you have brought an offering to your God; it shall be a statute forever throughout your generations in all your dwellings.
>
> **[F]** And you shall count *Mimahorat haShabbat*, from the day that you brought the sheaf of the wave offering; seven Sabbaths shall be complete; To *Mimahorat haShabbat haSh'vi'it* (the next day after the seventh Shabbat) shall you count fifty days; and you shall offer a new meal offering to Hashem.
>
> **[E]** You shall bring out of your habitations two wave loaves of two tenth deals; they shall be of fine flour; they shall be baked with leaven; they are the first fruits to Hashem.

[D] And you shall offer with the bread seven lambs without blemish of the first year, and one young bull, and two rams; they shall be for a burnt offering to Hashem, with their meal offering, and their drink offerings, an offering made by fire, of sweet savor to Hashem.

[C] Then you shall sacrifice one kid of the goats for a sin offering, and two lambs of the first year for a sacrifice of peace offerings.

[B] And the priest shall wave them with the bread of the first fruits for a wave offering before Hashem with the two lambs; they shall be holy to Hashem for the priest. And you shall proclaim on the same day, that it may be a holy gathering to you; you shall do no labor in it; it shall be a statute forever in all your dwellings throughout your generations.

[A] And when you reap the harvest of your land, you shall not make clean riddance up to the corners of your field when you reap, nor shall you gather any gleaning of your harvest; you shall leave them to the poor, and to the stranger; I am Hashem your God.

A. Note that the first substantive verse (10) uses the root *q-tz-r* (harvest) three times - it is not mentioned again until the final verse (22), where it is used four times. This total of seven times indicates that the *Milah Manhah* in this particular Parashah is *q-tz-r*, and that is entirely fitting, as even a cursory read of the Parashah will confirm.

C. The offering, while different, includes (at least) one lamb.

D. Both of these sections detail the wine libation and grain offering which accompany the offering.

E. The common use of *Mosh'voteikhem* and *Lechem* is surely not coincidental here.

F. These two verses are almost mirrors of each other - both entail counting, the phrase *Mimahorat haShabbat* and the number seven.

Of what use is this graphic representation and "structural discovery"? The astute reader will notice that I've skipped letter B – for therein lies our solution.

In the later occurrence of B, we read: "And you shall proclaim *B'Etzem haYom haZeh* (on the same day)" – referring to the proclamation of the Festival of Shavu'ot. This is "matched" with the first occurrence of *Mimahorat haShabbat* in v. 11. Perhaps if we can identify some significant allusion in the phrase *Etzem haYom haZeh*, we may be able to discern the Torah's intent in the use of this enigmatic phrase to describe the 16th of Nisan.

There are several occasions where the Torah uses the phrase *B'etzem haYom haZeh* (on that selfsame day) - when No'ach is brought into the ark (Bereshit 7:13), when Avraham performs B'rit Milah on himself and the males of his household (ibid. 17:23, 26) and the day when Moshe died (Devarim 32:48). None of the dates of these "selfsame days," however, is known to us. There is one notable exception - the phrase appears three times in Shemot 12 (vv. 17, 41, 51) describing the day of the Exodus. Unlike the other occurrences, that is a day which we can pinpoint with ease – the fifteenth of Aviv (Nisan). The only day which the Torah refers to (in narrative) as "that selfsame day" that belongs to a known date is the fifteenth of Nisan. (Analysis of the later application of this phrase to Yom haKippurim in Vayyikra 23, along with the occurrence of *Etzem haYom haZeh* in reference to the tenth of Tevet [Yehezqe'el 24:2] are beyond the scope of this shiur.)

By "matching" the first occurrence of *Mimahorat haShabbat* with *Etzem haYom haZeh* via the chiastic structure of our Parashah, we can easily see that the Shabbat in question is none other than the only *Etzem haYom haZeh* which we can associate with a known date – Nisan 15, the date of the Exodus.

V. Postscript

Subsequent to compiling this analysis, I was reminded of the famous passage in the *Sifri*:

> In three places it states *b'Etzem haYom haZeh*. In reference to No'ah it states it, because their generation was saying "we sense him planning such and such; we will not allow him [to enter the Ark]; moreover, we will take chains and axes and break his ark." The Omnipresent One said: "I will bring him into the Ark at midday and anyone who has the power to stop Me will come and do so.
>
> Why does it say, referring to Mitzrayim, "*b'Etzem haYom haZeh*"? Because the Egyptians were saying: "They are planning such and such, if we sense them [making an attempt to leave], we will not let them; moreover, we will take spears and swords and kill them. The Omnipresent One said: "I will take them out at midday and anyone who has the power to stop Me will do so."
>
> Why does it say here [in reference to Moshe's death] *b'Etzem haYom haZeh*? Because Yisra'el were saying "He is planning such and such; if we sense [that He is about to take Moshe], we will not let Him take the man that took us out of Egypt, split the sea, brought us the Torah and the *Mahn*, the quail and performed all of the miracles." The Omnipresent One said: "I will bring him into the cave at midday and anyone who has the power to stop Me will do so…" (Bereshit 47:9 adds a fourth instance - Avraham's B'rit).

In light of the ferocious dispute which revolved around the parallel phrase *Mimahorat haShabbat* and in light of the above passage from *Sifri*, the phrase *b'Etzem haYom haZeh* takes on added meaning: The proper day for the Omer-offering is the 16th of the first month – let anyone who [thinks that he] has the power to stop it come and do so! The declaration of Shavu'ot takes place "on that very day," protests of the Sadducees and their Boethusian allies notwithstanding.

Remaining Inspired by Routine Activities[1]

Rabbi Ralph Tawil

Value: Remaining Inspired by Routine Activities

The routine of religious observance is one of the pitfalls of organized religion, as opposed to the freshness of spontaneous religious experience and expression. On the other hand, if we were to wait for the religious experience to occur in a spiritual vacuum, we could be waiting for a long time. The spiritual person, who is a part of an organized religion, must find ways of infusing spirituality into the routine. This is the art of living inspired in every activity, not only in religious practice. Infuse new life into the routine. A midrashic comment on one word in our perasha informs this approach.

Background: After the miraculous exodus from Egypt and defeat of the Egyptian army at the Reed Sea, and after surviving hunger, thirst and enemies, Israel came to Sinai with God's assistance. There, it was about to experience a unique event in history—the revelation at Mount Sinai. The power of this event left an indelible mark on the spirit of Bene Yisrael. In the verse that begins the chapters describing the build up to the revelation, an unusual word draws midrashic attention.

Text: Exodus 19:1

> On the third month after Bene Yisrael went out of the land of Egypt, on this day (*bayyom hazzeh*) they came to the Wilderness of Sinai.

---

[1] Reprinted with permission from Rabbi Tawil's *Shabbat-Table Talks: Volume I* (New York: Tebah Educational Services, 2013) pp. 69-72.

Rashi: This was on the New Moon. Scripture should have written, "On that day" (*bayyom hahu*), why did it write "on this day?" [Scripture wanted to teach us that] the words of the Torah should be new for you as if they were given today.

Analysis: The straightforward explanation of the verse does not really make this point. It merely points out that on that very same day that was mentioned, Israel had arrived in the Sinai Wilderness. The Midrash notices an interesting anomaly and derives a beautifully true value from it. The verse referring to that day in the past should have used the more common word for distant reference. The use of the word of closer reference allows the Midrash to make its point. Since this whole section is the preface for the giving of the Torah, the Midrash is able to relate the idea that the revelation contained in the Torah should be as excitingly novel to you as if it were given today, and not a text that was given to our people over three thousand years ago.

Discussion: Read the verse and Rashi's commentary on the verse. Explain to your children that Rashi's comment is, in fact, a Midrash and that the straightforward (*peshat*) explanation of the Torah is merely that they arrived on that very day of Rosh Hodesh to the wilderness. Explain the importance of the Midrash as a way that our sages connected important ideas, values and even laws, to the verses of the Tanakh.

What does the Midrash mean when it says that the words of the Torah should be as new in our eyes as if they were given today? (You can explain this idea by using an example that your children will relate to. How do you feel when you get a new toy? You can't wait to play with it and even when you cannot play with it, like when you are in school, you are thinking about when you will play with it again. We should feel the same way about Torah. Even though we have learned that section already, or have done that *miṣvah* many times, each time it should be as excitingly new as if we were given to us this day.)

How can we treat it as new when it is really very, very ancient? The Torah has many deep principles and messages that apply to all times. These principles and their application to new situations that face us become more apparent to us when we are in situations that require a new Torah answer. In addition, as we grow older we can understand more of the Torah's wisdom and relate it to events in our own lives. (I recently reread a modern-day Torah book that I was unimpressed with when I first received it as a gift seven years ago. This time I was very inspired by the book's insights and wisdom. It is amazing how much the book had changed in seven years!)

The Torah has many *miṣvot* that we do every day, for example, prayer. How can we pray the same thing every day and be inspired by it? ([1] Although the prayer is the same every day, we are not. When there are certain aspects of the prayer that relate more to what we are experiencing these have more meaning for us. [2] Take the time to focus on the deep meaning of the words of the prayer—even if it means going slower. Remember, prayers are not a race to the finish line, but a reflective time in our lives when we focus on what is truly important to us as Jews. [3] Add some things in your prayer that reflect what is happening in your life. If it is important to you, pray about it. Since we always have different important things happening in our lives, our prayer can always be new.)

Another example is with Shabbat. Although Shabbat comes every week, and has the same basic structure, there are many different ways of experiencing Shabbat that are well within the framework of the *halakha*. One could think of the constant *miṣvot* as providing the framework within which many different things can happen. If Shabbat is getting boring for you, change the nature of your Shabbat activities to something else that is within the *halakha*. For example, if you are bored with a Shabbat that is comprised of praying, eating, sleeping and then some more praying eating and sleeping, followed by praying and eating, then change it; change the way and place where you pray, with whom you eat and skip some of the sleeping and enjoy the company of family and friends; spend some time in a Torah class; read an inspiring book; converse with friends etc. There are many ways of making the day inspiring within the framework.

By analogy, when we play basketball, the rules are the same, but every game is unique and sometimes exciting. Likewise, things that have a basic, unchanging framework can still contain many diverse experiences.

We can apply this idea to many other *miṣvot* and other aspects of our lives, for example, the people in our lives that we see and speak to every day. Have we taken the time to think about how our parents, spouses, children, or teachers are special? What are their unique qualities? What do I want to know about them? A little reflection about the important (and not so important) people in our lives can lead to deepened relationships and more inspired living—even within the common routine.

I once heard a song from a film that made a similar point of how to live inspired by life. The refrain of the song said, "Each time is the first time." The character sings that he plays the bouzouki (a Greek guitar) and that "you can't imagine how often I have played the bouzouki, but each time is the first time." Relish each moment with the people that we know and the opportunities to do *miṣvot* as the first time we are doing it and preserve the freshness of the Torah as if it were given this very day.

Megillat Ruth and the Shoftim Period[1]

Rabbi Alex Israel

The reading of the Book of Ruth is one of the beautiful customs of Chag HaShavuot. It is a picturesque and emotive story, and each year we are swept up, yet again, in the familiar yet exciting drama. We tensely follow the destitute Naomi and Ruth as they walk through along the roads of Moav, through the harsh landscape, deeply concerned for their fate. We watch excitedly as Ruth picks the gleanings from the field, hoping that someone will ensure that she brings home enough food at the day's end. We share the anticipation as we wonder whether Ruth will indeed marry Boaz and be able to set up a happy Jewish family, bringing the tragedy of the past to a brighter future; and indeed this is a story with a happy end.

However, I am not sure whether we realize quite how unusual and revolutionary the book of Ruth is. I think that if we examine this story in the light of its historical backdrop – the period of the Shoftim – and the book that parallels it – Sefer Shoftim – we shall understand how the message of Megillat Ruth is surprising and novel.

Megillat Ruth begins with the phrase: "And it came to pass, in the days of the Judges." Chazal suggest that the both the Book of Judges *and* the Book of Ruth were authored by the same individual – the prophet Shmuel. Two books describe the same period. And yet, I would suggest that the books differ radically.

---

[1] The following article is available on Rabbi Israel's website at http://www.alexisrael.org/#!shavuot-ruth-and-sefer-shoftim/cf2c.

I. The Shoftim Period

The period of the Judges lasted for over three hundred years. This period was a very difficult one for the young Israelite nation. Throughout these years, the country was repeatedly overrun by alien oppressors, neighboring states looking to expand their borders and to take advantage of the weakness of the Israelite nation. But these were not bad times simply from a military or national perspective. We can delineate at least four areas in which the Shoftim period was a disaster.

1. The fragile national security situation

As we have mentioned, the book of Judges talks about an entire collection of adversaries: Assyria, Moab, the Canaanite king Yavin, Midyan, Amalek, Ammon, the Philistines. The enemy intruders destroy the crops and commerce of the country, oppress and tax, and generally squeeze the Israelites to a situation in which normal life was unbearable. These phenomena occur nationally throughout the country; there is no region which does not suffer, at one time or another from the national weakness. When one enemy subsides, another arises.

2. The nature of the Judge-leader

Despite the existence of certain Judge-leaders, the primary characteristic of the time is the absence of a coherent **national** leadership structure.

The "Judges," as they are known, were ad-hoc leaders, individuals who rose to greatness by responding to the need of the moment. Invariably, the leader for any particular crisis situation emerged from the tribe which found itself at the epicenter of the problem or crisis. All of the "judges" are connected to military success. They always fight in the name of the God of Israel. But they are very much the transient heroes of the moment. In the same way that they rise to leadership and fame out of nothing, they fade rapidly into oblivion as a leading force in their tribe, or the nation as a whole. After their passing, they leave no successor and no continued leadership structure.

It is not too difficult to realize that the problems of national security would not have been nearly as acute had there been a leader with a national agenda and vision. A national leader can have a standing army that will act as deterrent to potential invaders. A figurehead gives the nation a focus, an identity. Central government can plan, can coordinate the resources and actions of a state on a macro level. Maybe a useful way to demonstrate the difference between the power of a Judge and a national leader is to note that in the wars that the Judges fought, the army never exceeded 40,000 fighting men. In contrast, King Saul, the first national leader manages to summon 330,000 soldiers in his first campaign (I Samuel 11:8).

3. Low spiritual level

This period is characterized by a powerful attraction to foreign deities. The most popular gods would have been the *Ba'al* and the *Ashtoret*, the gods of Canaan, but others were served as well. In the Tanach, it is this turning away from the God of Israel, their "straying" after pagan culture, which angers God, leading Him to remind them of His presence by subjecting them to oppression and national failure.

4. Inter-tribal friction

The nation does not see itself as a single cohesive unit in the period of the Judges. Frequently, tribes of Israel would simply fail to come to the assistance of their beleaguered brethren. Sometimes there are outbursts of inter-tribal violence, or civil war.

The problems of this era, as we can see, were enormous, complex, and not easily solved.

II. The Perspective from Sefer Shoftim

On the one hand, Sefer Shoftim blames the ills of the era upon the sin of *Avoda Zara* (Idolatry). It describes a recurring cycle of events, as follows:

1. Israel sins, serving other gods, local deities like *Ba'al* and *Ashtarot*.
2. God delivers them to their enemies.
3. They cry out ("moan" [2:18]) to God
4. He appoints a leader to save them and keep their allegiance to God.
5. The leader dies and they return to stage 1.

In other words, God punishes the people for abandoning His service. The lack of national security is a direct outgrowth of the lack of religious commitment of the nation.

But, on the other hand, Sefer Shoftim is also aware of another cause:

> "In those days there was no king in Israel and every man did as he pleased." (Judges 17:6, 18:1, 19:1, 21:25.)

In other words, there is a political cause and also a religious explanation for the abysmal state of the nation. Looking at Sefer Shoftim, one realizes that the solution lies in transforming both of these areas.

III. The Book of Ruth

Megillat Ruth describes the same reality but from a very different vantage point. Chazal suggest that Elimelech left the country due to the hardships faced during this period. People abandon a country in times of famine and violence. Apparently this family had the means to live abroad and to survive there, deciding to become refugees rather than face the frequent invasions and foreign occupation in Eretz Yisrael.

Megillat Ruth is the civilian side of the conflict, in which families become refugees and people are unwilling to assist their families because they are frightened for their own future. It is a time when Jewish life is far from certain or secure. Rather than taking the national vantage point, a grand sweeping vision of things, Megillat Ruth tells a personal story, a story of a single family that has to survive the torment that is swirling around them.

As we know, the move abroad did the family no good. Elimelech and his sons all die. And now Naomi is left alone and penniless. (Chazal once again attribute this to their leaving Eretz Yisrael.)

But how is the problem solved? Through kindness and charity!

- Ruth's kindness to Naomi (2:1).
- Boaz's consideration of Ruth (2:19, 21).
- Ruth's devotion to Boaz (3:10).
- Boaz's commitment to Elimelech (4:14, 9).
- Ruth's fulfillment of her commitment to her dead husband (4:10).

The way in which one reaches redemption in the story of Ruth is through *Ḥessed*, living up to life's responsibilities, caring for those around us, thinking beyond ourselves.

It is quite remarkable that Shmuel wrote two books about the period. In the first, he suggests that the nation will be saved through a religious transformation and through an organized central government. In this regard

Shmuel acts as a true statesman, attempting to guide the course of national events.

But in his second book, he suggests a radically different direction, suggesting that through small but heroic acts of kindness, one may change the world, one may induce redemption. Moreover, one may lead the way to the birth of King David himself! Just through simple but heartfelt acts of kindness and responsibility! Public policy is the arena of the nation, and yet, here we see actions on the personal and familial scale.

In this book, the verb *ga'al* – meaning "Redemption" – appears 24 times! That is quite a high frequency for a short book. Ruth is a book of Redemption, and Redemption is the small kindnesses that people perform for one another.

IV. In Conclusion

Shavuot is strongly centred upon the *Bein Adam Lamakom* (between Man and God) dimension of things. After all, it is on this "*zeman matan torateinu*" that we celebrate the eternal covenant enacted at Mt. Sinai. At that historic moment in time, we agreed to be a "kingdom of priests and a holy nation," and God responded with revelation and Torah. When Chazal describe the *Ma'amad Har Sinai* (the assembly and revelation at Sinai) as a wedding, they encapsulate the essence of things. It is not the particular Torah that we received on this day that is our focus. Rather, on this day we mark the fact that we as a nation became eternally tied to the Almighty by means of Torah.

And so, our Torah reading discusses the account of the Revelation at Sinai. The Haftara discusses the Revelation of Yechezkel in which the prophet Yechezkel was given a revelation of God's "*Merkava*," witnessing the angels, fire and sounds that surround God's presence. This day then, is about God's revelation.

Against this backdrop, Megillat Ruth comes as something of a surprise. Ruth is not a story of revelation. It is a very human story with deep human yearnings, fear, insecurities, and kindness, consideration and responsibility. It is a *Bein Adam Lechavero* story. Once again: where is the thunder and lightning and angels and fear? How does Ruth fit into the landscape of Shavuot?

It could be that Megillat Ruth is the *most appropriate* dimension of Shavuot. After all the Torah never specifies that Matan Torah happened on 6th Sivan. But it is *explicit* in Vayikra chapter 23 that Shavuot is a time for caring for the poor. There – in the paragraph that details Chag HaBikkurim – it states:

> And when you reap the harvest of your land, you shall not reap all the way to the edges of your field, or gather the gleanings of your harvest; you shall leave them for the poor and the stranger: I am the Lord your God. (Vayikra 23:22)

If there is *one thing* that we know about Chag Hashavuot, it is this description. When the Torah directs our attention to the Shavuot, it is focussed upon the harvest. And in thinking about the harvest, the Torah wishes to ensure that we are fully aware of the laws that apply at harvest time, laws that have the poor and disadvantaged at the forefront of their attention. And hence, might we suggest a very radical message for Megillat Ruth? That God is revealed in impressive spectacles, thunder and lightning, but God is also manifest in the small, sensitive acts of kindness that we can all do for one another.

Reflections on Megillat Ruth[1]

Rabbi Moshe Shamah

I. Introduction

Megillat Ruth is a superbly crafted short story possessing all the elements of great literature. Cast in a charming, idyllic setting, its characters, artfully and astutely portrayed, engage in deft dialogue with nary an extra word. While sparing of descriptive detail, it is replete with rich, potent allusions to profound notions. It contains dramatic use of tension in situations dealing with major decisions in life, in scenes that shift from subtle expectation to disappointment and finally to felicity. Its messages are often underpinned with subtle references to scriptural contexts and concepts. On the surface it is an example of God's reward for righteous behavior, specifically that of kindness and loyalty, and illustrates how with such behavior one may rise from the most humble state to royal heights, providing thereby an important message of universal import.

The Megillah also possesses a metaphoric dimension that transmits hope and inspiration to a nation in despair. The latter was very possibly the reason for its composition and inclusion in Scripture, a matter we shall discuss later in the study.

On the basic narrative level, the Megillah describes the trials and tribulations of Ruth, a young Moabite woman who was widowed from a Judean man who had been living in her country. Her husband along with his parents and brother had relocated to Moab from Bethlehem in Judah

---

[1] Reprinted with permission from Rabbi Shamah's book, *Recalling the Covenant* (Hoboken, NJ: Ktav, 2011), pp. 1067-1075.

because of a famine in their hometown. After about ten years, all three males were deceased and her mother-in-law, Naomi, decided to return home. Ruth, a woman of excellent character, possessed a remarkable degree of love and devotion to her widowed and bereaved mother-in-law. The Megillah depicts her courageous, unwavering decision to forsake her Moabite family, nation and god in order to remain with her mother-in-law and join Israel and its God, despite the significant hardships and stigma that were involved in doing so. This was an exceptional decision as she had not had any children.

Although not a word is said concerning her personal considerations in making such a life-altering decision, one cannot ignore the message transmitted between the lines. Clearly, Ruth had a Moabite family to which she could have returned, as Naomi – who surely was familiar with her family situation – continually advised, even urged, her to do. But she obviously had been deeply and compellingly impacted by the family she married into, despite the fact that it had separated from its patrimony and intermarried with Moabites. In light of the problems she would be expected to face as a Moabite in Israel, her choice is an impressive testimony to her appreciation of the merit of Israel's heritage, essentially its God and His laws. As Boaz remarked concerning her decision, referring to her relationship with the God of Israel, "May Hashem reward your deeds…that you have come to take refuge under His wings" (Ruth 2:12). Ultimately, she is rewarded with marriage and progeny from which Israel's national royal family stems.

In illustrating how the most glorious outcome may result from humble and alien origins, provided there is sincerity, goodness and perseverance, the Megillah is an important commentary on the Torah. Underlying the narrative is the theme of God's behind-the-scenes involvement, influencing events to help the righteous succeed in pursuing their worthy goals. But there is much more as we shall discuss in due course.

II. Allusions to Abraham and Yishaq

Ruth's extraordinary comportment is given fuller meaning, indeed, momentous significance, by the author's rich allusions to events in the lives of Abraham and Isaac. Parallels are drawn between God's לֶךְ-לְךָ ("go forth") call to Abraham to leave his father's home to proceed to the promised land – the foundational test crucial to Abraham's selection to establish the nation of Israel – and Ruth's doing so. The account of divine providence at work in Abraham's servant finding the appropriate wife for Isaac is the backdrop to Ruth's meeting Boaz and the preliminaries that eventually lead to their marrying. We will survey the linkage, pointing out how extensive it is.

God's selection of Abraham entails the challenge of taking leave of land, kinfolk and father's home to go to a land he does not know but one that God will direct him to, לֶךְ-לְךָ מֵאַרְצְךָ וּמִמּוֹלַדְתְּךָ וּמִבֵּית אָבִיךָ אֶל-הָאָרֶץ אֲשֶׁר אַרְאֶךָּ (Gen. 12:1). Ruth's decision to attach herself to Naomi contains similar elements and is described in strikingly comparable language. When Naomi tried to dissuade her daughters-in-law from accompanying her from Moab to Judah, she said: לֵכְנָה שֹּׁבְנָה אִשָּׁה לְבֵית אִמָּהּ ("Go, return, each woman to her mother's home" [Ruth. 1:8]). As a woman speaking to women to return home, the more emotionally laden "mother's home" is substituted for the more technically correct "father's home." Ruth's response includes אֶל-אֲשֶׁר תֵּלְכִי אֵלֵךְ ("Wherever you go I shall go" [v. 16]) recalling לֶךְ-לְךָ.

She continues with a comprehensive commitment to the nation of Israel and its God, corresponding to Abraham's response – silent but nonetheless salient – in hearkening to the divine call to go to a land he does not know. Later,

Boaz strikes similar notes in commending Ruth: וַתַּעַזְבִי אָבִיךְ וְאִמֵּךְ וְאֶרֶץ מוֹלַדְתֵּךְ וַתֵּלְכִי אֶל-עַם אֲשֶׁר לֹא-יָדַעַתְּ ("You left father, mother and land of your birth and moved to a nation you did not previously know" [2:11]).

When Abraham's servant, while on his mission to find a wife for Isaac, arrived at his destination, he was נִצָּב, "standing watchfully" at the well from which the town's young ladies drew water. He beseeched God, הַקְרֵה-נָא לְפָנַי הַיּוֹם וַעֲשֵׂה-חֶסֶד עִם אֲדֹנִי אַבְרָהָם ("Cause it to occur before me this day and do kindness with my master Abraham" [Gen. 24:12]). When Rebekah appeared, her magnificent response to his request included: אֶשְׁאָב עַד אִם-כִּלּוּ לִשְׁתֹּת ("I will draw until they finish drinking"), quenching their thirst (v. 19). When the servant's character test – essentially looking for the traits of kindness and sensitivity – was concluded, he asked, "Whose daughter are you?" Immediately upon her answer – learning that she is from the right family – he gives her gifts. Each of these elements has a thematic or distinctive linguistic parallel in the corresponding Megillah scene.

When Ruth first went out to the fields to pick gleanings, וַיִּקֶר מִקְרֶהָ וְגוֹ' ("It chanced for her to come upon the portion of the field that belonged to Boaz" [Ruth 2:3]). Boaz asked his assistant הַנִּצָּב עַל-הַקּוֹצְרִים וְגוֹ' ("who stood watchfully over the harvesters, 'to whom does this girl belong?'" [v. 5]). (In the following verse the foreman is again mentioned as הַנִּצָּב עַל-הַקּוֹצְרִים.) Immediately upon being told of Ruth's family connection, Boaz, having previously heard of her beneficence, begins extending great kindness to her. He tells her that when she becomes thirsty she may go to the vessels וְשָׁתִית מֵאֲשֶׁר יִשְׁאֲבוּן הַנְּעָרִים ("and drink from where the lads draw" [2:9]), introducing the linkage of both a water-drawing site as well as a thirst-quenching gesture into the narrative.

Abraham's servant gave thanks to God: בָּרוּךְ ה'...אֲשֶׁר לֹא-עָזַב חַסְדּוֹ וַאֲמִתּוֹ ("Blessed is Hashem...who has not forsaken His kindness and truth from my master" [Gen. 24:27]). He states his appreciation that God led him to his master's brethren. Although his mission still required great effort to bring the indicated result to fruition, God had spoken and the servant realized it; he now focused his efforts on bringing about the marriage. Meanwhile, Rebekah goes home and reports to her family (לְבֵית אִמָּהּ ["her mother's home]) what transpired (v. 28).

Ruth returns to her mother-in-law and relates the day's events. Although there is a long way to go, Naomi immediately senses divine providence at work and the matrimonial and redemption potential for her daughter-in-law, which she must still nurture with great skill in order for it to be actualized. She expresses her thanksgiving to God with the following words: בָּרוּךְ הוּא לַה' אֲשֶׁר לֹא-עָזַב חַסְדּוֹ ("Blessed be he to Hashem who has not forsaken His kindness" [Ruth 2:20]). It is noteworthy that these Genesis and Ruth usages of the phrase אֲשֶׁר לֹא-עָזַב חַסְדּוֹ are the only two attestations of this locution in Scripture. Naomi then proclaims that God has led Ruth to a relative, קָרוֹב לָנוּ הָאִישׁ מִגֹּאֲלֵנוּ הוּא ("The man is related to us, he is from our redeemers"), using words very similar to those of Abraham's servant when he acknowledges that God has led him to take the daughter of אֲחִי אֲדֹנִי ("my master's brother") for Isaac. In redemption contexts, "redeemer" and "brother" are employed virtually synonymously (see Lev. 25).

Ruth added a detail: Boaz had also told her, "Stay close to my young men until they conclude all my harvest" (Ruth 2:21). He employed the identical phrase Rebekah did when informing the servant that she would draw water until the camels were through drinking: עַד אִם-כִּלּוּ ("until they finish"). Individuals of good character complete the task or responsibility of kindness they began. Again, these are the only two attestations of this locution in Scripture.

Upon the servant being seated in the home of Rebekah’s parents, he made a point of his desire to expedite his responsibility: “I will not eat until I speak my words” (Gen. 24:33). When Naomi senses that Boaz recognizes his responsibility, she comments that, “the man will not be quiet until he concludes the matter today” (Ruth 3:18). It is also praiseworthy to be prompt in fulfilling a responsibility one has accepted.

Finally, when Isaac marries Rebekah, the Torah states, וַיִּקַּח אֶת-רִבְקָה וַתְּהִי-לוֹ לְאִשָּׁה (“[Isaac] took Rebekah and she became his wife” [Gen. 24:67]). When Boaz and Ruth marry, it states, וַיִּקַּח בֹּעַז אֶת-רוּת וַתְּהִי-לוֹ לְאִשָּׁה (“Boaz took Ruth and she became his wife” [Ruth 4:13]). These are the only two attestations in Scripture of this compound phrasal formula. Both words of the succeeding phrase in the Megillah, וַיָּבֹא אֵלֶיהָ (“and he cohabited with her”), are alliteratively linked to the immediately preceding phrase in that corresponding Genesis verse, וַיְבִאֶהָ יִצְחָק הָאֹהֱלָה (“and Isaac brought her into the tent”).

With this full constellation of correlations the message is unmistakable. Ruth was a sincere convert to the nation of Israel; she sensed God’s call, following in the footsteps of Abraham (and Rebekah). As God intervened on behalf of Abraham to provide the proper wife for his son so did He on behalf of Naomi, to provide the proper husband for her daughter-in-law. Things come about in ways that to the casual observer might appear as happenstance but to the discerning eye are providential. Superlative virtues distinguished both Rebekah and Ruth. As Isaac and Rebekah deserved each other so too did Ruth and Boaz, and a notable future such as had materialized for the former couple was in store for the latter one.

III. The Moabite Connection

Awareness of the Torah legislation regarding Moabites is seemingly necessary to fully understand certain facets of the Megillah.

> An Ammonite or Moabite may not enter the congregation of Hashem (קְהַל ה'); even unto the tenth generation they may not enter the congregation of Hashem, ever, because they did not come forward toward you with bread and water when you were on the journey coming out of Egypt and for hiring against you Balaam…to curse you. (Deut. 23:4-5)

The Talmud limits the prohibition to males, one interpretation being that it is essentially the males' responsibility to come forth with bread and water to weary travelers and another being that the terms עַמּוֹנִי וּמוֹאָבִי imply males (Babylonian Talmud *Yebamot* 76b-77a). Since the logic of making a distinction between males and females was not so apparent, this permissibility for females was variously contested and not fully accepted in all places at all times. The Talmud, in its *aggadic* fashion, asserts that at one point it was necessary to threaten force to have the distinction accepted (ibid.).

Upon deciding to return to Bethlehem, Naomi had endeavored to discourage her daughters-in-law from joining her by referring to the difficulty of marriage. She may have been alluding to the potential problem related to the concept ensconced in these Deuteronomic verses. When Naomi and Ruth entered Bethlehem, the whole town buzzed with surprise over them. However, contrary to the general practice in human society when a bereaved and needy widow returns home, there is no indication of any significant befriending of them. Undoubtedly, this was because of the Moabite stigma.

Although Boaz was greatly impressed with Ruth and encouraged her to remain in his fields, provided for her protection from molestation, and allowed her privileges not accorded the other poor, in certain ways he remained aloof. He did not inform her of his being a close relative of her late father-in-law even upon discovering her connection to Naomi. He did not relieve her of the necessity to stand all day in the sun gathering gleanings so that she and her mother-in-law could survive. He made no effort to contact Naomi, and took no initiative regarding redemption of the land. Despite his compassionate expressions these were disappointing omissions; based on the refusal of the closer redeemer (Ruth 4:6) we may assume that they resulted from his fear of the Moabite connection.

It appears that Naomi's awareness of Boaz' fear explains why, at the end of the season, when she realized Ruth's contact with Boaz was about to conclude, she advised her to take matters into her own hands. She sensed that it was necessary to present Boaz with a powerful and clear-cut opportunity to face up to his responsibility and take the appropriate action, even if the only tactic available bordered on seduction. Her tactic recalls Tamar's strategy with Judah (Gen. 38). Oftentimes, even high-quality individuals are victims of fear and inertia and do not address matters of social justice that lie within their immediate sphere of human interaction until they are directly challenged, at which time they rise to the occasion.

When the relative closer than Boaz was informed that the condition of redeeming Elimelech's property involved marrying Ruth to establish the deceased's name on his property, he backed off, expressing the fear that it will ultimately damage his estate. He was presumably concerned that the law concerning a Moabite may one day be thought of as prohibiting marriage to Ruth. Boaz declared his willingness to redeem the land and marry

Ruth. He called the elders and others to witness his intent and there was a large, public ceremony to confirm the transaction. The halakhah was firmly established that his marriage to Ruth was permitted and everybody extended blessings.

Boaz' name means "in whom is courage." He took the correct stand in accepting Ruth, although it may have been unpopular and although he knew that it would require ongoing steadfastness in the future.

IV. Another Aspect of Meaning

Additionally, the Megillah is a tale of a family's resurrection after having almost reached the point of obliteration. During a famine a man with his wife and two sons left Bethlehem of Judah to live in Moab. The singular and anonymous וַיֵּלֶךְ אִישׁ ("a man went"), following the general tone of the previous clause informing of a famine in the land, indicates that he left while others were not leaving Judah. We later discover that this man, Elimelech, possessor of a distinguished name meaning "my God is king," had been a landowner from a prominent family. Moving to Moab, he abandoned his heritage and people. He soon dies. His wife Naomi, "pleasantness," is left with the sons, Mahlon and Chilion, names meaning "sickness" and "destruction" respectively. Obviously these are symbolic names, for people do not so call their sons. Indeed, all the Megillah's names appear to be symbolic.

Both sons marry Moabite wives and after about ten years they also pass away, childless, leaving forlorn widows. All that remained of the family were the bereaved mother beyond child-bearing years and her two Moabite daughters-in-law. Upon Naomi's urging, Orpah returns to her family, her name apparently referring to the "back of the neck," derived from her action of turning away. The family that abandoned its spiritual legacy is now practically decimated, a significant statement about the negative consequences associated with leaving the land of Israel.

Nevertheless, the Megillah teaches, as long as there is life there is hope and redemption is possible. The restoration was brought about in a way impossible to have imagined – through the superlative loyalty, kindness and sacrifice of the remaining Moabite daughter-in-law, Ruth.

In the Talmud (*b. B. Bat.* 14b) the view is expressed that Megillat Ruth was written by the prophet Samuel, at the end of the era of the judges (pre-1000 B.C.E.), relatively close to the time of its setting. However, the literary evidence indicates that it was composed some centuries later. It states, "Thus was the custom in former times in Israel…to validate a transaction, one man would take off his shoe and hand it to his fellow" (Ruth 4:7), implying it was written in an era when the old custom not only fell into disuse but was widely unknown. The Megillah's opening verse, "And it was in the days when the judges ruled" (1:1), is more suitable for an author living after the time of the judges, describing a time long past. While the Megillah's language is classic biblical, some of its diction and word usage appears more consistent with the exilic period, such as the words *te'agena* (1:13), *vayiṣbot* (2:14), and others. Rabbi Solomon D. Sassoon was of the opinion that it was probably written about the time of the Babylonian exile of Judah in 586 B.C.E., part of the prophetic works of Jeremiah. At that time, the national situation was bleak with the people deep in despair and in great need of encouragement to counteract their pessimism and prompt them to believe that there was hope for restoration.

The severe decline and near elimination of the family may very well be an allegory referring to the nation of Israel going into exile, beset by the enormous trials and tribulations that befell it there, tottering on the verge of extinction. In that case, the family's resurrection would refer to the amazing national revival and restoration of Israel when a small part of the remnant chose to sincerely commit itself to the covenant. Although the principles of repentance and return are detailed in the Torah, theoretical statements benefit from a story manifesting the principles at work. Indeed, when reading the last portion of the Deuteronomy execration section predicting the final chastisement in the land followed by exile with tremendous problems continuing there (Deut. 28:59 ff.), one cannot help but think of the two sons who died prematurely and childless, מַחְלוֹן וְכִלְיוֹן ("sickness" and "destruction"). That Deuteronomy 28 text explicitly speaks of sicknesses with the words חֳלָיִם and חֳלִי (vv. 59, 61) followed shortly afterwards by וְכִלְיוֹן עֵינַיִם ("a wasting away of the eyes" [v. 65]).

Rabbi Sassoon understood the name רוּת (Ruth) as cognate with the Aramaic word יְרוּתָא ("inheritance"), corresponding to the Hebrew word for inheritance, יְרוּשָׁה, consistent with the rules of שׁ and ת transference between these languages. Thus, the heroine's name appropriately strikes the theme of the message. It is noteworthy that on the Moabite Stone (9th century B.C.E.), the word for יְרוּשָׁה is written with a ת (see *Natan Ḥochmah Lishlomo*, pp. 101-102).

V. Ruth and Tamar

As pointed out, Ruth's sincerely motivated clandestine attempt at union with Boaz (Ruth 3:9) recalls Tamar's sincere deception of her father-in-law Judah (Gen. 38), from which Perez, Boaz' paternal ancestor, derived.

There is unmistakable structural and conceptual linkage between the Genesis narrative concerning Tamar and the narrative of Ruth. At the head of the families are Judah and

Elimelech. Judah separates from his brothers and home locale, marries a Canaanite woman and has sons (three), two of whom die prematurely and childless. Elimelech leaves his land with his two sons who marry Moabite women and who also die prematurely and childless. In both narratives carrying on the name of the deceased through the available widow – *yibbum* (levirate marriage) or redemption – becomes a central theme of the narrative as well as a primary goal of the female protagonist. The males, however, postpone or avoid it. Judah wrongly fears possible death for his remaining son through contact with Tamar, while Elimelech's relative fears marriage with Ruth, which may "destroy" his estate, probably because of the Moabite connection.

At a critical point, when it appears that *yibbum* or redemption will be put off indefinitely, the women act boldly. Tamar is told that Judah will be going to shear his sheep, a traditionally joyous time for sheep owners, presenting her an opportunity. Ruth is told that Boaz – Elimelech's relative who replaces him in the schematic plan – has concluded the harvest and will be winnowing his crop, a similarly joyous occasion, comparable to the sheep-shearing. At a time when Tamar knew Judah was vulnerable (having been consoled upon the death of his wife), she removes her widow's clothing, dresses for the occasion, and stations herself for her task of seducing Judah in a location where he cannot help but notice her. Ruth bathes, anoints herself, dresses appropriately and uncovers Boaz' sleeping blanket and slips under it at his feet. Tamar used deceit while Ruth employed stealth.

Judah yields to the temptation and Shelah, who was the more appropriate *yabam*, is pre-empted. The progeny that derives from that liaison includes Boaz. Boaz, on the other hand, exercises self-restraint – "she lay at his feet until morning" (Ruth 3:14) – explaining to Ruth that there is one relative closer with whom the primary rights and responsibilities reside. (Rabbi Sassoon thought this should be viewed as representative of Boaz correcting Judah's impetuousness.) When the first-in-line refuses to exercise his right Boaz rightfully marries Ruth. The blessing of the people and the elders includes, "And may your house be like the house of Perez whom Tamar bore unto Judah" (4:12). From that relationship derives King David (v. 17).

VI. General Remarks

As a Moabite, Ruth derived from Lot's liaison with his elder daughter (Gen. 19:37). Thus, King David, who derived from Boaz and Ruth, had these formative "illicit" relationships on both paternal and maternal pedigree lines. The wife of David's son Solomon, the mother of Rehoboam, through whom the royal line was carried forward, was Naamah the Ammonitess (1 Kings 14:21), a descendant of Lot's liaison with his younger daughter (Gen. 19:38).

That the royal line of Israel derives from such relationships teaches that a background of lowly birth does not relegate an individual to an ignoble life. Divine providence comes down on the side of purity of heart when joined with ongoing compassionate, altruistic and innocent intentions, as opposed to favoring the strict letter of the law.

In an interesting comment on the long reign of King David, in contrast to the much shorter one of King Saul, talmudic sages state: "We do not appoint a *parnas* over the public unless a קֻפָּה שֶׁל שְׁרָצִים ('a basket of rodents,' signifying questionable background) is hanging from behind him, so that if he becomes haughty and arrogant, we can say to him 'look at your background'" (*b. Yoma* 22b).

Rabbi Hiyya points out that every verse in Ruth begins with the letter *vav* except for eight, a feature which he takes as an allusion to Ruth's deep attachment to the covenant (*Yalquṭ Shim'oni*, Ruth 608). Whether this statement was intended as *peshat* or not, the number eight (as well as its decimal multiples) does signify the covenant (see our study "On Number Symbolism in the Torah," p. 1057). It surely is noteworthy that the Megillah proper (excluding the five-verse epilogue which is a genealogical addenda) is composed of exactly eighty verses.

Regarding the custom to read Ruth on Shabu`ot (cited in *Massekhet Sopherim* 14:16), the following may be said: Since on that day we celebrate the nation's entering into the covenant, it is appropriate to read the inspiring story of an extraordinary individual who recognized the great value of sacrificing in order to be part of Israel and its heritage. It is also heartening to read of the magnificent reward God bestowed upon her. In addition, on this auspicious occasion it is proper to remind ourselves that the heritage of Israel is open to all sincere individuals who genuinely accept the responsibilities of the Torah, regardless of national or genealogical background, and that based on their personal merit they may rise to attain the foremost eminence within the nation.